To Kill A Mockingbird

Harper Lee

Guide written by Stewart Martin

A Literature Guide for GCSE

Contents

Contents

Plot summary

1 The story is set in the mid-1930s in Maycomb, a small, isolated, inward-looking town in Alabama, USA. The narrator is Scout Finch, who looks back to when she was a young girl living with her brother Jem and their father Atticus, a lawyer. Their household is looked after by Calpurnia, a stern but kind Negro woman, because the children's mother died when they were very young.

7 As a punishment for destroying Mrs Dubose's camellias, Jem has to read every day for a month to this cantankerous dying neighbour. After Mrs Dubose's death, Atticus tells the children that she was a brave woman who died having won her painful fight with an addiction to painkillers. On a visit to Calpurnia's church, the children learn more about Tom Robinson.

2 At Scout's first day at school we meet some of the children of the long-established local families, like the Cunninghams and the Ewells.

6 The children learn new respect for Atticus when he shoots a mad dog, and they discover that he is known in the town as an expert with a rifle.

9 The trial of Tom Robinson takes place amidst strong feelings in the community, especially when Atticus demonstrates that Tom is probably innocent by questioning the girl, Mayella Ewell. It is clear that she has lied about the rape, but after long consideration by the jury, Tom Robinson is found guilty.

8 Aunt Alexandra comes to stay. There are difficulties when she tries to make the children behave as she thinks proper and when she tries to get Atticus to sack Calpurnia.

Scout and Jem, together with their new friend Dill, try to get a mysterious neighbour who has not been seen for 15 years – Boo Radley – to come out of his house. Atticus disapproves of their activities, because he is trying to bring his children up to be tolerant and he thinks they are pestering Boo. Although Boo has a frightening reputation amongst the local children, he leaves Scout and Jem presents hidden in a hole in a tree outside his house.

4 During a cold winter night, a fire burns down their neighbour's home and, unknown to Scout, Boo puts a blanket round her shoulders to keep her warm.

Atticus is to defend Tom Robinson, a Negro man accused of raping a white woman. This causes tension with some of the white townspeople, many of whom are deeply prejudiced and racist.

10 The girl's father, Bob Ewell, spits at Atticus and threatens trouble in the future. Tom Robinson tries to escape from prison and is shot 17 times.

11 On their way home from a Halloween pageant one dark night, the children are attacked with a knife by Bob Ewell and Jem is badly hurt. During the fight, Boo Radley comes to their aid and Bob Ewell is killed. The sheriff persuades Atticus to pretend that Bob Ewell fell on his knife.

Scout

The story is narrated by Scout, who is six at the beginning and nine when the story ends. The language of the book is adult in style, because Scout is recounting memories of her childhood. Interestingly, the book is set in the 1930s and Harper Lee would have been seven in 1933. She is therefore contemporary with Scout. Scout is a lively, intelligent, astute girl who prefers boyish activities. She has a strong will and a hot temper which gets her into trouble with adults. She dislikes school intensely and lets her feelings be known to the teacher. Scout has a close relationship with her father, who tries to make her use her head instead of her fists. Before the trial she is taunted by the other children because Atticus is defending a Negro. Her instinctive reaction is to physically fight back but, swallowing her pride, she obeys her father and refuses to retaliate. Scout's wild behaviour and frank speech offend Aunt Alexandra, who feels Scout should become more 'ladylike'. Scout resists these attempts to make her more feminine, preferring the openness of male company to the sly suggestions made by her aunt's companions.

Scout's character changes as she begins to learn how to look at things from another person's point of view. <u>Just as her father says, she learns to step into another person's shoes and walk around in them.</u> She learns to understand the feelings of Boo Radley and of her aunt too, and also to respect the changes in Jem. She has great sympathy for Mayella Ewell and for her friend Dill, and is quite without prejudice. Having a child's mind and approach to life is often shown in the novel to be an advantage; the situation outside the court-house, when Atticus faces a lynch mob, is a good example of this. The children learn by experience that adults are not always right, and Scout illustrates the importance of developing an open and unprejudiced mind of one's own. She decides early in life that no matter how other people seek to divide up the human race into different sorts or types of people, there is really 'just one kind of folks. Folks.'

Jem

The story begins when Jem is ten and finishes when he is thirteen. The development of his character is traced as he approaches adolescence. At first, Jem enjoys normal childhood pursuits like playing football, inventing games, and amusing himself with his friends. As the story unfolds, Jem becomes more moody, is less willing to join in games with Scout and their friend Dill, and prefers to be on his own. He is milder tempered than his sister Scout, and more sensitive to other people. Jem is four years older than Scout and this is reflected in his attitudes and reactions. On several occasions, the author allows us to see Scout trying to guess Jem's thoughts. This narrative technique reveals a great deal about both Scout and Jem. A good example of this occurs in Chapter 7, when the children find the two carved soap figures in the Radley's tree.

Only on one occasion does Jem explode into anger – when he knocks off the tops of Mrs Dubose's camellias. As a result of this incident he learns a lot about personal courage. He is told by

Atticus, when Mrs Dubose dies, that true courage is not a man with a gun, 'Its when you know you're licked before you begin but you begin anyway and see it through no matter what'. Tom Robinson's trial is also a very significant event in Jem's growing up. He is devastated by the unjust verdict and it takes him a long time to come to terms with the imperfection of people. Atticus explains to him that by it taking the jury a few hours to reach a verdict, they have accomplished a small victory in making people less prejudiced in the future. At the same time, Jem's awareness of the feelings of others increases and he finally understands that Boo Radley stays indoors because he wants to, not for all the sinister reasons the children had imagined earlier. Jem develops a keen sense of responsibility, which is shown when he seems to break the childhood code of secrecy and informs Atticus of Dill's presence at the Finch house. He becomes more protective towards his sister, and develops a tactfulness and a way with words that reminds us of Atticus.

Atticus

Atticus Finch, fifty years old and a widower, is the father of Jem and Scout. With the help of Calpurnia, the cook, he is raising the children on his own. He stands out as a man of reason and courage. In the face of the prejudice and strong emotions of the people of Maycomb he tries to make his own children see that it is better to use one's head than to resort to fists or, even worse, to guns. Atticus shows considerable bravery in defending Tom Robinson, knowing the likely unjust outcome of the trial. He is driven by a strong belief in the equality of people before the law, and although he fails this time to gain a just verdict it does not diminish his faith in the law. As he remarks in Chapter 11: 'before I can live with other folks I've got to live with myself. The one thing that doesn't abide by majority rule is a person's conscience.'

His children are disappointed that Atticus doesn't play football or poker, and that he neither drinks nor smokes. Atticus is described as old and short-sighted. On the other hand, he is an expert marksman and a man to be relied upon. The people who matter in Maycomb hold Atticus in very high regard.

Atticus is subjected to criticism from his brother and sister because of the way he brings up his children. Although he gives Jem and Scout considerable freedom, he demands high standards of courtesy, honesty and good manners from them. He is very fair with them and will always listen to both sides of any argument. He represents the voice of truth and fairness in the community – notice Dolphus Raymond's opinion of him in Chapter 20. Miss Maudie says of him, 'We trust him to do right.'

Atticus's philosophy of life is expressed early in the novel when he says to Scout: 'You never really understand a person until you consider things from his point of view ... until you climb into his skin and walk around in it' (Chapter 3). Despite his virtues, Atticus is not unapproachable. He is a popular man with a keen sense of humour. But Atticus is not perfect. His faith in the goodness of man leads him to underestimate Bob Ewell, with almost fatal consequences. His other mistake, in thinking that there are no lynch mobs in Maycomb, might also have resulted in death had it not been for Scout reminding the men that regardless of their differing viewpoint, that they were all human beings, living side by side in the same town. She does this by discussing Mr Cunningham's son Walter with him.

Boo Radley

Arthur Radley, or Boo as the children call him, is a figure of fear and mystery at the beginning of the story. He was locked in the house by his father for stealing a vehicle and then resisting arrest fifteen years before.

He is a monster, ghost or 'haint' in the minds of the children. ('Haint' probably comes from the French 'hanté', which means haunted.) The children learn that when he was thirty-three years old he calmly stabbed his father in the leg with a pair of scissors and had to be locked up in the courthouse basement.

The community's fear exaggerates his activities to include poisoning pecan nuts in the schoolyard, eating cats and squirrels raw, terrifying Miss Crawford by staring through her window at night, and killing azaleas by breathing on them.

Boo gradually emerges as a very different sort of person from the one the children imagine him to be. When items appear in the tree outside his house, the children realise he is leaving them gifts. When Jem has to abandon his torn trousers on the Radley fence, they reappear mended. When Scout is watching the fire at Miss Maudie's house, Boo covers her shoulders with a blanket. Boo's greatest act of kindness is coming to Jem and Scout's aid when they are attacked by Bob Ewell, even though this involves Boo in killing a man with a knife. It is only then that they actually meet Boo for the first time. He is very different from the monster of their imagination, or the man described by Stephanie Crawford in Chapter 1. He is a gentle, quiet, and very shy man.

Calpurnia

Calpurnia is more than just the family's cook. She is a replacement mother. Her firm control over the children causes Scout to resent her. Atticus trusts and supports Calpurnia entirely. When Aunt Alexandra wants to get rid of her, he is firmly against it. Calpurnia is intelligent and is one of the few Negroes in Maycomb who can read and write. She leads a 'double life', partly amongst white people and partly at home with her fellow Negroes. This is shown most clearly when the children accompany her to church and see her within her own community (Chapter12). They are surprised when they learn that she talks differently amongst her own people. Calpurnia is very down to earth in her explanation of this. People have got to want to be educated themselves. You cannot force them. If they do not want it, there is no point flaunting your own education.

Maudie Atkinson

Miss Maudie is the children's favourite neighbour. She is popular with them because she treats them with kindness and respect. She genuinely likes their company, bakes them cakes and, most importantly, does not talk down to them. Miss Maudie is a very individual character, who shows courage by holding views different from those of other people in Maycomb. When the strict sect of Baptists criticises her for growing flowers, she matches their biblical quotations with others from the same source. Miss Maudie is quite philosophical about losing her house in the fire and cheerfully carries on with life. She is critical about people's motives when they go to watch Tom Robinson's trial, calling it a 'Roman carnival.' She knows that at the trial a verdict of guilty is inevitable, but she sees grounds for optimism, even though she thinks the verdict is wrong. She explains to the children that a small step along the path to true justice has been taken. She has a sharp tongue and is not slow to use it when faced with the hypocrisy of the ladies at the missionary tea. Scout admires and respects her for this. Together with Atticus, Miss Maudie represents the voice of reason amongst all the fears and prejudices of the town. Her attitude towards hypocrisy can be guessed from the way she reacts in Chapter 24, when Mrs Merriweather criticises Atticus. Miss Maudie says acidly: 'His food doesn't stick going down, does it?'

Tom Robinson

Tom Robinson is a 25-year-old black man who is falsely accused of rape by a white woman. He is married with children and is a hardworking family man. In Chapter 9 it becomes apparent that Atticus is going to defend Tom and that the town does not approve of this. Scout is taunted by a boy from school and later, in Chapter 15, a lynch mob waits at the jail to administer vigilante justice on Tom Robinson. Fortunately this is averted, and when the case is heard in court it becomes increasingly apparent that Tom Robinson could not have raped Mayella Ewell. This is because the right side of her face is bruised and Tom's left arm has been crippled since childhood. Also, there is no way he could have hit her, held her down and raped her with the use of only one arm. He has, up until this accusation, been as respected as a black man could have been at this time. He is clearly held in high esteem by his employer and the black members of the town. The fact that during his trial he is honest enough to admit to feeling sorry for Mayella Ewell and claims that she made sexual advances towards him, angers the racist members of the community. Sadly he is found guilty and in an attempt to escape is shot dead. Seventeen bullet holes were found in him and it is tragic that he would have escaped had he had the use of both his arms. Atticus explains Tom's decision to run by saying, 'I guess Tom was tired of white men's chances and preferred to take his own'.

About the author

Harper Lee

Nelle Harper Lee was born on 28th April, 1926, in Monroeville in southwestern Alabama, about halfway between Mobile and Montgomery. She was the youngest of three children, and her father was a lawyer who also served on the state legislature from 1926–38. Her background is almost exactly the same as that of Jean Louise Finch (Scout): born in 'Maycomb' (in the next county to Monroeville), the younger of two children, whose father is a lawyer. It is widely believed that the character of Atticus was based on Lee's father and that as a child Lee was just like Scout. She was a tomboy and an avid reader, enjoying the company of the now famous author Truman Capote, upon whom she admitted basing the character of Dill.

During Lee's childhood there were a series of trials that perhaps influenced the inclusion of the trial of Tom Robinson in *To Kill A Mockingbird*. These were the infamous 'Scottsboro Trials', which began in April 1931 when Lee was a mere five years old. Nine African American men from the little town of Scottsboro in Alabama were falsely accused of raping two white women. It became apparent during the legal process that there was medical evidence that proved that these women had not been raped. Nevertheless, the all-white jury found the men guilty and all but the youngest, who was aged twelve, were sentenced to death. As with Tom Robinson, the men only just survived long enough to face trial, having almost been the victims of a lynch mob. Unlike Tom Robinson, over the years all but one of the men were either freed or granted parole.

Harper Lee read law at Alabama State University, but six months after graduating in 1950 she left to go to New York, with the hope of becoming a writer. During the 1950s she gave up the job she had taken in New York (with Eastern Airlines as a reservation clerk) and concentrated on full-time writing. Her father became unwell, causing her to split her time between her home town and New York. In 1957 her first manuscript was submitted for publication, but she was urged to rewrite it. The publishers felt that it read like a series of short stories, and Lee worked at integrating these stories into what is now a very famous literary work. It was finally published as *To Kill A Mockingbird* in 1960. The book met with instant critical and popular success: within two years it had won four literary awards, including the Pulitzer Prize. The novel sold over 15 million copies and in 1962 it was made into a film starring Gregory Peck. As a full-time writer, Harper Lee returned to Monroeville. *To Kill A Mockingbird*, despite its success, remains her only novel. The remarkable international success of the novel has brought her financial security, and yet Lee has given very few interviews, preferring to live a quiet existence, dividing her time between New York and Monroeville. She has had several essays published in magazines and journals.

The summary above suggests the extent to which Harper Lee identifies with the characters and setting of *To Kill a Mockingbird*. The mixture of pride in the South's history and values and shame at its racism is not unusual among Southern liberals. Alabama was admitted to the Union in 1819 and played a momentous part in the Civil War of 1861–65. The Civil War was fought over the secession (breaking away) of Southern slave states from the rest of the United States to become the Confederate States of America. The reason for secession was the North's opposition to slavery, so the war was fought (and lost) by the Confederacy on the issue of slavery. Novels such as Harper Lee's *To Kill A Mockingbird* emphasise the ongoing racist attitudes that continued to exist in the American South, where the small-town white communities perceive the black community as inferior. Consequently, it is impossible for Tom Robinson to receive a fair trail and, as with others before him, he is falsely convicted of rape. Harper Lee shows the reader, through the character of Atticus, that such miscarriages of justice will only cease when the individual person rather than their colour is put on trial.

Alabama was called 'the cradle of the Confederacy' and Montgomery, Alabama, was the first capital of the Confederacy. (Later, Richmond, Virginia, became the capital.) It is impossible to understand 1930s Alabama without reference to slavery, the Confederacy and the Civil War. You will find that *To Kill A Mockingbird* is full of Civil War generals' names: Braxton Bragg, Hood, Stonewall Jackson ('Ol' Blue Light' – not to be confused with Andrew Jackson who had earlier driven out the Indians). Harper Lee herself shares a surname with the greatest of all Confederate generals, whose name appears in the character Robert E. Lee Ewell.

At the end of the Civil War the Emancipation Proclamation freed the slaves and briefly, in the period of Reconstruction, the Negro population had equality and power. This period lasted a mere twelve years, and soon blacks were excluded from government, segregated from whites and generally treated as inferior. In the period after the First World War the Ku Klux Klan was active, terrorising blacks and their sympathisers with lynchings and burnings. At the time of the events in *To Kill a Mockingbird* things were made worse by the Depression: nationwide economic collapse and high unemployment which President Franklin D. Roosevelt was attempting to improve with his New Deal policies. The Depression hit the poorest hardest.

In the 1950s, when Harper Lee was writing this book, Alabama was again at the centre of racial tension. Martin Luther King worked as a minister in Montgomery from 1954, and it was there that his Civil Rights work started, with the Montgomery bus boycott which de-segregated the town's buses in 1956. In the early 1960s, Ku Klux Klan outrages were reported in Montgomery and Meridian, Mississippi, Dill's home town.

Maycomb, as created by Harper Lee, is a 'tired old town' where little happens, though dangerous prejudices and tensions are always there. In Southern states, such as Alabama, belief in the literal truth of the Bible is widely held, and many people in the novel are strict Baptists or Methodists. Most of the characters are good according to their own standards, but these standards are narrow (in 1925 a teacher in neighbouring Tennessee was prosecuted for teaching the theory of evolution). It is a static population and newcomers (even from North Alabama!) are not accepted easily. Gossip is rife, and so is prejudice. Not only are blacks subjected to racial prejudice, but any person who in any way fails to conform is treated as odd: for example the Radleys, or Dolphus Raymond. Most of all, things change very slowly: what was so in 1861 is still important in 1933. These things were also still important when Harper Lee was writing in the 1950s and, to some extent, are still important now.

Courage

We can recognise several kinds of courage in the book. There is the basic courage required to overcome childish fears, such as running past the Radley place. Atticus shows the same kind of physical courage in facing the mad dog. A more difficult form of courage is the moral courage that Scout has to find in order not to retaliate when her friends call her father names. The most difficult form of courage to possess is the courage to take on and carry through a task which is certain to end in failure. Atticus has to do this when he defends Tom Robinson. Mrs Dubose also chooses to do this, when she attempts to rid herself of drug addiction (she knows she is dying and, in that sense, there is no point to her battle). She wins her fight, and Atticus calls her 'the bravest person' he knows. Atticus wants the children to realise that courage is not 'a man with a gun in his hand'.

Bob Ewell is a man totally without courage. He tries to take revenge on the children, and even then he does not have the courage to face them in daylight, but strikes in the darkness. Boo Radley shows courage when he rescues the children.

Family

Because of the static nature of the Maycomb population, the same families have lived in the area for nearly two hundred years. As a result, some people feel that each family seems to inherit particular characteristics. They can say that a Cuningham can always be trusted or a Ewell is always dishonest. This leads to social division: every family is categorised on a particular scale and it is important to mix with the 'right' family. Aunt Alexandera is particularly prone to this kind of snobbery. Atticus is against this kind of social classification, preferring to judge a person on individual merit.

The Cunninghams are a family of very poor farmers who live in Old Sarum in the north of the county. They act mainly as a contrast to the Ewell family. The Cunninghams never borrow what they cannot return and they pay their bills promptly, even if they have to pay in vegetables rather than money.

It is thanks to a Cunningham that the lynch mob disperses at the jail. Scout recognises Mr Cunningham and by talking to him about family matters, she makes him think like an individual again and not like a member of a mob. Finally, thanks to another Cunningham, the jury is delayed in returning their verdict. This delay gives both Atticus and Miss Maudie grounds for optimism for the future of their society.

The importance of having family to look after and guide you is also demonstrated through the close relationship between Atticus and his two children. He, along with Calpurnia, spends a fair amount of time with his children instilling good values in them. This directly contrasts with the Ewell family life, where Mayella has been totally responsible for looking after her younger siblings since the death of her mother.

Justice

In theory, all American Negroes have had equal rights in law since the end of the Civil War in 1865. Yet that does not always mean they receive equal justice. The court's verdict against Tom Robinson, shown through Jem's trusting, inexperienced eyes, emphasises this. Atticus upholds his belief that the law is satisfactory. The law can function, but justice cannot be carried out until attitudes change. It is people who must apply the law justly.

Prejudice and hatred

The deep hatred and fear that exists between Whites and Negroes in the novel means that violence could break out at any time. The lynch mob, made up of normally reasonable, respectable men, is ready to kill and nearly succeeds. Bob Ewell's hatred of Atticus nearly results in the deaths of Jem and Scout. Although circumstances force him to use his gun, Atticus does not want his children to admire violence. By pleading for tolerance, Atticus hopes to show the children how the causes of violence can be removed. Atticus is perhaps too idealistic here, because he misjudges the extent of Bob Ewell's hatred.

A dominant theme in the novel is the cruelty that people inflict upon others by the holding of pre-formed ideas, 'the simple hell people give other people', as Dolphus Raymond puts it. These ideas are not simply deep racial prejudice, but also the intolerant, narrow, rigid codes of behaviour that the townspeople of Maycomb wish to impose on each other. This bigotry (another word for prejudice) is made all the more menacing by being depicted as 'normal' behaviour by many characters in the book. Against this background, people such as Boo Radley, Dolphus Raymond and, to some extent, Maudie Atkinson, are persecuted because they do not conform. Tom Robinson is found guilty even though it is strongly suspected that his accusers are lying, because he went against the 'acceptable' behaviour of a Negro and dared to feel sorry for a white person.

So deeply entrenched is racial prejudice in Maycomb that the townspeople do not realise their own hypocrisy. The author highlights such double standards during Aunt Alexandra's missionary circle tea. The women talk with great sympathy about the plight of the poor Mruna tribe in Africa, but later condemn the dissatisfaction of the Negroes in their own town.

Dolphus Raymond is also regarded as an oddity in the town, because he is a white man who chooses to live amongst Negroes. He is a sensitive man who loathes the society which makes black and white people live separately. The only representative of black prejudice is Lula, but the church congregation controls her behaviour and makes her outburst ineffective. The blacks resent Tom's conviction but as they have been second-class citizens from birth, they seem to expect it.

The mockingbird

The image of the mockingbird occurs frequently in the book. The children are warned that it is a sin to kill this bird because all it does is sing. It has no original song of its own, but merely copies the songs of other birds – hence its name. Tom Robinson and Boo Radley are both gentle people who have done no harm but only try to help others. Like the mockingbird, Tom and Boo should be protected and cared for. Instead, they are hunted down by the mob, who are full of false courage, ignorance and shallow pride – like the children who shoot songbirds. Both Tom and Boo are persecuted, one by the jury and the other by the children and the gossips. The mockingbird symbol links to two important themes in the book: justice and childhood. Justice is 'killed' when the jury follow their own prejudices and ignore the true evidence. The innocence of childhood dies for Jem, Scout and Dill when they realise that the adult world is often a cruel and unjust place.

Text commentary

Chapters I to 7

Chapter 1

> **❝*When he was nearly thirteen...*❞**

The narrator's age at the time of the story is important. Because it allows the novel to take advantage of two different viewpoints which are years apart, and this gives a more complete picture of events. <u>The story is narrated by the adult Scout, looking back on her childhood and her feelings at the time the story is set.</u> The story has a cyclical structure, as it begins by describing Jem's injury and ends after the events leading to Jem's injury have taken place.

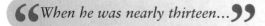

There is a strong sense of autobiography in the writing of this novel. The device of an older person retelling incidents from their childhood is not uncommon in literature, and it is used in *To Kill a Mockingbird* to good effect in two ways. Firstly, Scout often relates incidents that she does not fully understand, as happens in the case of Boo Radley, when Jem grasps – long before she does – that the items in the tree are presents from him to them. The reader can piece things together which Scout does not understand: this adds depth to the narrative. Scout's incomprehension also adds an element of humour. The second strength of looking at the story through a child's eyes is the impact it lends to the question of racial prejudice in the South. The injustice stands out because the children are aware of it for the first time.

> **❝*'He liked Maycomb, he was Maycomb County born and bred.'*❞**

Atticus was named after a Roman who lived from 109–32 BC. The Roman Atticus escaped to Greece during the Roman civil war. He refused to join either side in the civil war.

Why is this an apt name for the children's father? Look at Chapter 16 to get an idea of why this might be.

Explore

Look at the way the opening of the film *To Kill a Mockingbird* depicts Maycomb. It will give you a real sense of what the American South would have been like.

Read the opening part of Chapter 1 carefully. It has been suggested that Maycomb is based on Monroeville in Alabama, where Harper Lee's father, like Atticus, was a lawyer.

The importance of heredity and 'background' is a theme which runs throughout the book. We know that the Finch family have lived in this area for over a century. <u>So strong is the family network that different families have become recognisable</u> by definite characteristics. Thus the Haverfords are all jackasses, and the Cunningham and Ewell families have particular identities. This tendency to 'pigeon-hole' people is a part of the intolerance displayed by some characters in the novel. What does all this tell you about the likely attitudes of its inhabitants? Would you expect them to be narrow-minded or broad-minded? Notice how the children at the school have already acquired the values of their parents, and how it is this which causes their new teacher so many problems. Do people who are intolerant usually come from backgrounds where the adults are prejudiced also?

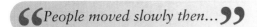

People moved slowly then...

Explore

To get more of an idea about what the depression was like, read John Steinbeck's *Of Mice and Men*, or watch the film version of the story.

The mid-1930s was a time of economic depression in America, especially in the South. The only hope that things might improve came from Franklin D Roosevelt, elected President in 1932, who offered Americans a 'New Deal'.

Text commentary

66Calpurnia was something else again...99

Although she is employed as the cook, Calpurnia's role in the family is obviously more important than that. Atticus shows total respect for Calpurnia and considers her to be part of the family. Judging from the narrator's comments that Calpurnia's hand was 'wide as a bed slat...' and that she was 'tyrannical', how do the children regard her?

Explore

It has been suggested that Dill was based on Harper Lee's childhood friend Truman Capote, who is most famous for writing *Breakfast at Tiffany's*.

Look at the direct way in which the children speak to each other. What particular qualities of the behaviour of children is the author conveying here? Consider what they say to each other about the subject of reading. What does Jem's remark, 'don't have any picture shows here' reveal about the backwardness of the town?

The importance of religion in the lives of the people of Maycomb is significant in the book, and it is interesting that Jem should point out that the only picture shows they ever get in Maycomb are 'Jesus ones'. It seems ironic that a group of such 'God-fearing' people should be so intolerant and prejudiced.

66Inside the house lived a malevolent phantom...99

The mystery of the Radley Place is not sensed merely by the children. It becomes, for adults too, the object of superstition and fear. The townspeople of Maycomb are shown to be more influenced by fear than by reason. The Radleys are regarded as strange and different because they do not conform to the rigid patterns of behaviour that the Maycomb people expect. They keep to themselves and do not really associate with the townspeople, thus making themselves a prime choice to gossip about. Mr Radley is described as a man who 'took the word of God as his only law'. It seems strange that he can behave so cruelly to his son and yet profess to be religious.

> **❝**Nobody knew what form of intimidation Mr Radley employed to keep Boo out of sight.**❞**

The innocence of childhood is shown in the way Jem thinks that Boo Radley must be chained to the bed to make him stay in all those years. Atticus's experience of life and people tells him that there are 'other ways of making people into ghosts'.

The cruelty of Mr Radley towards his son is underlined by Calpurnia's comment. Why is her condemnation of Mr Radley particularly significant? (Why do the children feel so surprised by her remark?) This is the first comment on the relationship between Negroes and Whites. Compare Calpurnia's behaviour in the white community with that when she takes the children to church and is surrounded by the black community.

Read Jem's description of Boo. It is a wonderful combination of imagination and reason. Children are credulous and will believe stories as long as the stories seem plausible and agree with what the children already think. <u>There is a great deal of fear and superstition regarding Boo Radley in the adult community as well. He has been built up to be some kind of insane monster.</u> The local people are similarly manipulated by speculation and prejudice during the trial of Tom Robinson.

There is some rivalry between Jem and Dill. What does Dill say that finally makes Jem put 'honour' before 'his head'?

Chapter 2

Jem and Scout are very close but, according to Jem, once they are at school their friendship must stay private. Like many children, Jem feels he must conform in public to the behaviour of his friends. There is no room for his sister, a girl four years his junior, in his circle of school friends. The pressure to conform can also be seen in the behaviour of the adults in the book. Only individuals with strong consciences, like Miss Maudie and Atticus, can free themselves from it.

> **❝Miss Caroline printed her name on the blackboard...❞**

Look at the strong influence of past events on people's attitudes. Miss Caroline Fisher is regarded with suspicion because of her origins; she comes from a part of Alabama that stayed loyal to the North during the Civil War. People have long memories – the story takes place **70 years after the Civil War.** North Alabama is seen as somewhere quite different from Maycomb because it is industrial, Republican and – most significantly – because people there have no 'background'.

Miss Fisher's 'foreignness' is emphasised by her choice of story. She does not appreciate that the majority of her children come from a background that makes them 'immune to imaginative literature'. **The word 'immune' shows that the people of Maycomb regard some things as so foreign, so threatening to their way of life, that they are comparable with disease.**

Harper Lee pokes fun at the public education system here, where a teacher scolds a child for having already learnt to do what it is her job to teach her. Miss Fisher behaves absurdly by telling Scout to stop her father teaching her, because it will interfere with her reading. Scout's sense of fairness is outraged because she does not understand what wrong she has done, especially as no one has really ever taught her to read.

The teaching system which Miss Fisher is attempting to put into practice is not, in fact, known as the Dewey Decimal System. Jem's error is an amusing confusion of the Dewey Decimal System used to catalogue library books (invented by Melvil Dewey) and the theories of the great American educator, John Dewey. The rigidity of the school system is shown when Scout is told she must print, not write, for the next two years. The lessons about current events falter because the majority of children come from homes where the newspaper contains few 'current events'. In all, Scout is not impressed with her first day at school. Are you?

❝ Miss Caroline, he's a Cunningham... ❞

Scout assumes that her teacher will understand the significance of this comment and that everybody in the world is like the people of Maycomb. This is a normal attitude in children but is also that of many of the Maycomb adults.

❝ My special knowledge of the Cunningham tribe... ❞

The Cunninghams are proud, honest, poor and very independent. They will not accept charity from the church or government, in contrast to the Ewells, who gladly receive help from the state. Part of the humour in the book stems from Scout's innocent enquiries and statements. Here, Jem teases her about the meaning of the word 'entailment'. (This is a legal term. It means placing restrictions on who can inherit land or property.) Scout obviously remembers the term – see Chapter 15.

We gain an insight here into the plight of the poor farmers in the South during the 1930s. Poverty forced them to mortgage their property or sign entailments. This meant they then needed hard cash to repay debts. The government offered work in the form of paid welfare schemes, but taking the work meant they would have to leave their farms. People such as the Cunninghams, who were a 'set breed of men', were reluctant to do this because it would mean seeing their property go to ruin.

"Miss Caroline stood stock..."

This is another example of humour arising from Scout's innocence and ignorance. She makes an incorrect assumption about why she has to put out her hand. What do you think of Scout's behaviour on this, her first morning at school? Has she been outspoken, or is she merely unaware of the behaviour expected of her? Whose fault is it really that she is punished?

Think about whether you have any sympathy for Miss Caroline and try to decide why school has been so difficult on the first morning. Is it simply that she is new to the school? To what extent do you think her problems are caused by her not being from Maycomb, but from Winston County, in North Alabama? It is clear that Miss Blount, a native Maycombian, seems to have certain advantages over her. Consider the children's attitude towards her and vice versa.

Chapter 3

"Catching Walter Cunningham in the schoolyard gave me some pleasure."

The difference in temperament between brother and sister is quite marked. Scout is hot-headed, and settles arguments quickly by the only method she knows – her fists. Jem is more reasonable. Look for similarities between Jem and Scout and their father. As Atticus is a widower, we cannot look for similarities between the children and their mother. Unlike Jem, Scout does not remember her mother clearly. So who do you think Scout becomes more like as she grows up?

The repartee between Jem and Scout is often very amusing. With the normal childlike desire for fairness and honesty, neither will let

the other get away with boasting, invention or lies. Look at how Scout deflates Jem's claims about his behaviour in front of the Radley Place.

Explore

The description of Burris's father as 'right contentious' (argumentative) is a forewarning of the dangers ahead. (See Chapters 23 and 28.)

<u>One of the greatest lessons that Atticus and Calpurnia try to teach the children is tolerance of other people's behaviour.</u> That is why Scout is so soundly scolded when Walter Cunningham comes to dinner.

Burris Ewell and Walter Cunningham are dressed very differently. Burris' clothes are filthy; Walter's are at least clean, if patched.

The need to look at circumstances from the other person's point of view is a strong theme in the book. It is the chief lesson Atticus teaches his children. He tries to make Scout see the day at school from Miss Caroline's point of view. Note how by the end of the novel Scout has learned to see things from other people's perspectives.

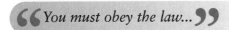

❝ *You must obey the law...* ❞

Explore

Why is bending of the law more possible in a small town than it might be in a big city?

Atticus points out that Scout must go to school as it is the law. The Ewells live entirely by their own rules. He explains that for three generations, the Ewells have been 'the disgrace of Maycomb'. The law is bent for the Ewell children, out of compassion.

Think about how everyone knows everyone else's business in a small town, and how this can lead not only to a kind of arrogance but also to humanity and compassion. (Look at what Reverend Sykes says to his congregation about Helen Robinson in Chapter 12.) How true is it that to know someone is to understand

Text commentary

them, as Atticus seems to believe? The Bible suggest that to understand is to forgive. At the end of the novel we might be able to forgive Mayella Ewell, but can we forgive her father?

Chapter 4

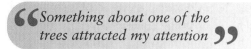
Something about one of the trees attracted my attention

Explore

Do you think Jem has connected the Indian-heads (one cent coins) with Boo Radley?

The children begin to find items left for them in the knot-hole in one of the trees in the Radley garden. First they are left chewing gum, then coins.

Here is an interesting gap between Scout the narrator, who understands the situation, and Scout the seven-year-old, who does not. Scout observes that, 'Before Jem went to his room, he looked for a long time at the Radley Place'.

Dill enjoys the superior position that travel and life in a bigger town give him. He boasts, too, of his father's position. However, Jem and Scout are not taken in by him. Why does Dill make up so many tales about his parents, his travels and his life in general? Is Dill essentially a lonely child?

What is the effect of saving until the end of the chapter the information that Scout heard someone laughing inside the Radley place? Scout's revelation suddenly adds drama and new meaning to something which has already happened in the novel. An important quality of the author's style is the way in which events assume a greater and often a different importance, the further we read. You, the reader, constantly change your understanding of things which happen, just like the children do. This technique – of revealing new slants on past events as time goes by – is also a skilful way of suggesting that the children are growing up.

Chapter 5

> **❝Dill was in hearty agreement with this plan of action❞**

The humour at the start of this chapter lies in the straightforward way Scout relates events and deals with situations. She still is very much the young child who feels that any argument can be settled with fists. She gradually grows away from this idea as she matures. The narrative shows both the naïvety of childhood and reflections made by the adult Scout in hindsight.

> **❝Miss Maudie hated her house: time spent indoors was time wasted❞**

Miss Maudie is sympathetic towards the children. She allows them a great deal of freedom in her garden, talks to them in a friendly way, and offers them cakes. She is contrasted with the frightening, intolerant Mrs Dubose and the gossipy and rather empty-headed Miss Stephanie Crawford.

The strict sect of Baptists that Mr Radley belongs to had quite an influence in the South. Their narrow views about good behaviour add to the already intolerant atmosphere of Maycomb, and Scout seems to grasp intuitively that these strict Baptists must be wrong in condemning Miss Maudie to hell for loving her garden. Scout appreciates Miss Maudie's goodness, even though she does not actually go about 'doing good' in public, as some characters do.

Miss Maudie's common sense makes her aware of the dangers of interpreting the Bible too literally. She fears that people like Mr Radley, who believe that they must strictly obey the laws of their religion, are hurting other people in the process. That, to her, is wrong. She says that these people are, 'so busy worrying about the next world they've never learned to live in this one…'.

Miss Maudie's comment is a central argument in the novel, and that is why Harper Lee shows so much of the children's education. <u>The children learn to 'live in this world' in a way which many adults in the novel cannot.</u> The educational system in Maycomb, as represented by the children's teachers, seems based on the assumption that 'projects' and 'units' are a good preparation for 'this world'.

Atticus's lack of hypocrisy is emphasised by Scout, and Miss Maudie agrees: 'Atticus Finch is the same in his house as he is on the public streets'. How many other people in the book are like Atticus, as regards their public and private behaviour? <u>Atticus is shown to be a genuine person who stands no nonsense, as can be seen at the end of the chapter when he tricks Jem.</u>

Chapter 6

In this strictly religious atmosphere, what do you think would be people's attitude towards gambling? Look at Miss Rachel's reaction to Dill's excuse that he and Jem were playing strip-poker. The gentle humour of the book surfaces again in Scout's innocent misunderstanding of the reactions of adults – because they all 'stiffen' she thinks that 'the neighbours seemed satisfied' with Dill's outrageous explanation.

Chapter 7

Scout is beginning to learn the lesson that Atticus has been teaching her. We do not yet know, however, why Jem is so moody. Scout assumes that it is a reaction to the terrifying experience of going back, alone, to the Radley Place at night. It is another example of how the reader does not yet know all the facts of the incident.

There's something I didn't tell you

Explore

Why is this behaviour so difficult for Jem to understand?

Jem finally deigns to talk to Scout and tells her about finding his trousers mended and hanging on the fence. The poorly mended trousers make Jem realise that it is probably Boo Radley who returned his trousers and is leaving the things in the tree.

<u>Jem is going through the painful process of discarding youthful assumptions and ideas which he has now discovered to be quite wrong.</u> This is something which Atticus, among others, is trying to persuade the people of Maycomb to do: discard their prejudice. Jem's inner development and growth is set in ironic contrast to the children's state education, whose achievements (teaching Jem about the Dewey Decimal System, and enabling him to walk 'like an Egyptian') seem wholly irrelevant to the real business of growing up.

Jem does not want Atticus to know where they found the things. Think about Atticus's reaction to their attempts to make Boo come out. Which things has Scout still not connected? <u>Notice how the narrator, although the same person as Scout, can make Scout appear ignorant of the facts that the reader can guess at.</u>

Explore

Compare Jem's reaction to what Dolphus Raymond says in Chapter 20 about the way people treat each other.

Jem realises that Mr Nathan Radley was lying about the tree. He had blocked it up deliberately. Think about why he might have done this and why it moves Jem to silent tears. Jem seems to understand more about what has been going on than his sister. This is <u>another skilful touch by the author which reminds us of the different levels of maturity of the two children.</u>

Text commentary

Uncover the plot

Delete two of the three alternatives given, to find the correct plot. Beware possible misconceptions and muddles.

Jean-Louise (Dill/Boo/Scout) and her brother John/Jem/Jack live with their father, Atticus, and their cook, Caroline/Maudie/Calpurnia, in Maycomb County, Alabama. It is the 1830s/1930s/1960s, and slavery/prejudice/economy, both racial and class-conscious, rages strongly. While Atticus practises criminal law/economy/tyranny the children spend their time at school and at play with their friend Walter/Burris/Dill. Their favourite game involves acting out the life of Arthur/Nathan/Chuck (Boo) Radley, a neighbour who has been shut away/dead/ill for so long that superstition surrounds him. As the game progresses (with Atticus's delight/disapproval/amusement) it becomes apparent that it is not going unnoticed by someone on the Finch/Crawford/Radley estate. During a night visit to the house, Jem loses his trousers: when he collects them they have been burned/stolen/folded and inexpertly darned. Small gifts are left in the knot-hole of a Radley oak, until Atticus/Boo's father/Boo's brother – claiming that the tree is dying – fills the hole with cement.

Who? What? Why? When? Where? How?

1   What does Scout think caused her father's 'profound distaste' for the practice of criminal law?

2   Where does Dill come from, and why does he come to Maycomb?

3   In what ways were the Radleys alien to Maycomb's ways?

4   How did Arthur's father view his son's sentence, and what was the result?

5   What can Scout do that – according to Miss Caroline – she shouldn't?

6   Who are 'the disgrace of Maycomb', and why?

7   How does Miss Maudie remember Arthur Radley?

8   What does Mr Radley 'shoot' in his collard patch?

9   When does Scout think she and Jem first began to part company, and why?

10 Why does Jem cry when Atticus says that the tree filled up by Mr Radley is not dying?

Chapters 8 to 11

Chapter 8

The snowfall in the night results in different kinds of humour. Scout's behaviour is funny because she over-reacts out of ignorance; there is the narrator's dry humour about the effects of sin; then there is Scout's innocent trust in all adult pronouncements. (The information about the Rosetta Stone is, of course, nonsense; this Egyptian stone inscribed with hieroglyphics had nothing at all to do with weather prediction!)

> **As it has not snowed in Maycomb since 1885, there will be no school today**

Eula May phoning the house with this information emphasises the smallness of the town. Look at the list of jobs entrusted to the town's telephone operator. Touches like this are continual reminders of the inward-looking nature of this isolated town. It takes a man two days to get from the north end of the county to Maycomb in order to obtain 'store-bought' goods, which is perhaps surprising when we recall that Maycomb was the centre of government for the county.

Explore

What does Atticus mean when he says 'Looks like all of Maycomb was out tonight in one way or another.'?

Jem realises who has put the blanket around Scout's shoulders. This is an example of real life contradicting the children's previously held beliefs. Why is Jem so anxious to tell Atticus all they know about Boo Radley? What does Jem now realise about Boo's character that Scout has yet to appreciate? To identify how she still sees him, study Scout's reaction when Jem mimics Boo approaching her with the blanket.

Miss Maudie's reaction to the destruction of her home tells you about her character. Why do you think Scout is surprised at her reaction? Miss Maudie seems to care more for her flowers than for her home, but in fact this is quite in keeping with her character. These are the things which she regards as most important in life. Can you explain why the loss of her house does not upset her more than it does?

Chapter 9

<u>Scout responds to Cecil Jacob's accusation that her father defends niggers with a display of physical violence.</u> This is the first mention of the trial and is introduced from Scout's point of view. Scout's frankness is funny. After her father's vain attempts to control her spirited behaviour she admits: 'I soon forgot'. For a young hothead like Scout, Atticus's lessons on tolerance fail to go very deep.

> **66** *every lawyer gets at least one case in his lifetime that affects him personally* **99**

The case of Tom Robinson is a matter of honour for Atticus. <u>He knows he cannot win, but he must take it on or lose his self-respect, the respect of his children and the respect of those townsfolk whose opinions he values.</u>

Atticus is certain he will lose the case because he knows exactly what the status of the Negro is in the South. In spite of the abolition of slavery at the end of the Civil War, Southern Negroes remained second-class citizens. They lived in a separate part of town, received inferior education, and had to take on the poorly paid jobs. Even in court they were not equal. This is why Atticus is so sure of failure.

Scout is beginning to remember to be reasonable, and for a few weeks she accepts being called a coward for the sake of her father. She is starting to grow up.

Atticus has a great sense of duty towards his family. He refuses to break the tradition of Christmas, even if some members of the family are tiresome to be with. This is important, because it demonstrates that even the tolerant Atticus has to work at keeping his feelings under control.

An important lesson that the children learn as they get older is that adults frequently have to do things which they would rather not do (for all kinds of reasons), and that they must do them properly. Examples of this are: persevering in the face of defeat; exposing liars; shooting dogs; visiting dull relatives. These are all done by Atticus.

Aw, that's a damn story

Scout's growing-up process leads her into the use of swear words. Atticus wisely ignores this latest trend as a passing fad, and it is her uncle who reprimands her. Atticus's tolerant attitude towards his children comes in for a lot of criticism from the family, especially from Aunt Alexandra.

Scout is a tomboy. If Jem wishes to insult her, he accuses her of behaving like a girl – as in Chapters 4 and 6. There is a vast difference between Atticus and Aunt Alexandra in their attitudes to Scout. Atticus lets Scout be as she is. Aunt Alexandra tries to make her dress and play as a girl, mistakenly believing that Atticus would secretly prefer Scout to be that way.

Explore

Do you think Atticus is right to adopt the approach he does, or is he simply being a poor father and spoiling his children?

I guess it ain't your fault if Uncle Atticus is a nigger-lover besides...

Most children have a well-developed sense of fairness and Scout is angry with her uncle, not for the beating but because he did not take the trouble to listen to her side as well. Scout has come to expect fair dealings because that is how Atticus has always treated his children. Contrast Scout's behaviour with that of Uncle Jack – the humour here comes from the way Scout seems to be telling him off. What has happened here to the usual positions of child and adult? Where else in the novel does this occur? (Look at the school scenes.)

Atticus understands children well. Firstly, he believes in honesty, because children know when they are not getting a straight answer. Secondly, he selects from their behaviour the things that need correcting (like Scout's hot-headedness) and ignores those things that are probably best ignored (like Scout's new-found interest in swearing).

> **❝I'm not worried about Jem keeping his head, but Scout...❞**

Atticus deliberately switches the conversation to the trial when he becomes aware that Scout is listening. This is because he wants her to hear what he is saying, and to think that she is overhearing it, rather than being told it directly. Atticus is clever here: you already know that Scout 'soon forgot' when he told her directly to do things.

Explore

What does Atticus mean by 'Maycomb's usual disease'?

Atticus sets himself apart from the people of Maycomb. He does not share their prejudice when it comes to Negroes, and he is realistic about his chances of changing their attitudes. He is afraid that this trial might damage his relationship with his children. Whose influence does he fear they may fall under?

Chapter 10

> **❝Shoot all the bluejays you want, but remember it's a sin to kill a mockingbird...❞**

When the children get air-rifles, <u>Atticus</u> <u>explains</u> <u>that</u> <u>it</u> <u>is</u> <u>wrong</u> <u>to</u> <u>kill</u> <u>something</u> <u>that</u> <u>does</u> <u>no</u> <u>harm</u>, and gives only pleasure with

Text commentary

its song. This is reinforced by Miss Maudie. Look at Miss Maudie's description of the mockingbird. As you learn more about the characters of Tom Robinson and Boo Radley, see how far you think they fit this description.

Why is talk of Atticus's limitations included at this point in the book? Does it diminish or increase his stature in the eyes of the children? How do the children eventually come to regard him?

Jem was stunned by the marksmanship of his father. Why do you think Atticus had kept his marksmanship a secret? Atticus is no longer proud of something which, when he was younger, he was extremely proud of. Jem cannot understand this immediately, but realises later that as people grow up their views of things change, provided they keep an open and tolerant mind. Scout's reaction is the very reason why Atticus kept quiet about his skill with a gun. He did not want his children boasting about his ability to kill. In contrast to Scout, Jem is mature enough to admire Atticus's silence.

Explore

Notice the children's change in attitude towards their father. Do they see him differently by the end of the novel?

Chapter 11

> ❝*Don't you say hey to me, you ugly little girl! You say good afternoon, Mrs Dubose!* ❞

Mrs Henry Lafayette Dubose is a neighbour of the Finches who frightens the children with her unkind remarks. She is introduced and dies in the space of one chapter, and through her the children learn an important lesson about courage.

Over the years she has become addicted to morphine, which she used as a painkiller because of illness, but she struggled at the end of her life to free herself from the addiction, even though she knew she was shortly to die. Without realising it, the children help her to achieve an important personal victory.

The children, in their uncomplicated way, have clear feelings about Mrs Dubose: 'Jem and I hated her'. However, she plays an important part in their growing up, and by the time of her death they realise it is wrong to judge others too quickly or too superficially. They might have admired Atticus for the wrong reasons if they had known about his skill with a gun. In the same way, they learn that people they might never dream of admiring can have admirable sides to their characters.

Jem and Scout are going to have to learn that one has to do what is right whatever other people think. To do that sometimes requires considerable courage.

Atticus tries to cool the children's indignation at hearing their father being called names. He tries to make them understand that such language reflects badly on the person who uses it, not on the person it is directed at. This is a difficult lesson for them to learn.

Explore

Relate what happens here to Atticus's cool, calm and collected response to Bob Ewell spitting at him.

Atticus tries to show his children the true meaning of courage. Mrs Dubose knew she was facing a painful task in breaking her drug addiction, with little chance of success. Her courage lay in making the attempt. The fact that she succeeded is actually not all that important, it simply demonstrates that sometimes it is possible to win such battles. Was Mrs Dubose's victory a pointless one, do you think? How courageous is Atticus in taking on the impossible defence of Tom Robinson? Do you think Atticus is simply being stubborn if he knows his stand will not make any difference in the end?

Quick quiz 2

Uncover the plot

Delete two of the three alternatives given, to find the correct plot. Beware possible misconceptions and muddles.

For the first time since 1785/1885/1985 it snows in Maycomb County. During the night, Atticus's/Miss Maudie's/Mr Avery's house catches fire; for safety, Atticus sends Jem and Scout to stand in front of the Radley/Crawford/Dubose house and, while they watch the fire, Boo/Nathan/Mrs Radley slips a blanket round Scout's shoulders. The children learn that their father is defending a Negro in a simple/uninteresting/difficult case and suffer taunts from their fellows. At Christmas they go to Finch's Landing to visit their Aunt Alexandra, and Scout ignores/fights/admires her cousin Francis for calling Atticus a nigger-lover. As the situation deteriorates, Jem and Scout are reminded of their father's qualities when he saves Boo Radley/Stephanie Crawford/the neighbourhood from a mad dog by shooting it expertly and humanely – they were unaware of his shooting skills. They are tormented by Mrs Dubose, a sick neighbour, and Dill/Scout/Jem loses his head and ruins her camellias. As a result he is forced to read to her until shortly before her death, learning afterwards that with great courage she had fought and beaten her addiction to reading/camellias/morphine.

Who? What? Why When? Where? How?

1   Why does Atticus say he doesn't know if Jem will become an engineer, a lawyer, or a portrait painter?

2   What does Atticus rescue from Miss Maudie's house?

3   What main reason does Atticus give Scout for his decision to defend Tom Robinson?

4   Why does Francis spend each Christmas at Finch's Landing?

5   Who 'ain't fair', and why?

6   How did Atticus come to be given the Tom Robinson case?

7   Why is it a 'sin' to kill a mockingbird?

8   Why does Atticus no longer hunt?

9   When does Jem lose his temper?

10   According to Atticus, what is the one thing that doesn't abide by majority rule?

Quick quiz

43

Chapters 12 to 21

Chapter 12

Explore

Notice how even Scout, who is a confirmed tomboy, is eventually forced to conform to behaving like a girl. How does she rebel against this?

Jem is growing up, and Scout finds it hard to accept the changes in him. He indicates that he does not want their relationship to continue as before. Jem is coming under pressure from his classmates. This is a small-scale example of the social pressure that exists in Maycomb. Isn't this how intolerance and prejudice begin?

Jem and Scout are made to feel unwelcome by Lula because they are white. What point is the author making here about racial prejudice in the South? Does it work only in one direction?

Scout watches what is going on in the church with curiosity, comparing and contrasting this service with those in the church she usually attends. She is free from preconceived ideas about a Negro church, and this is reflected in the fascinated way she describes it.

❝He's just like our preacher...❞

The children's innocence shines through here. They have not yet become aware of the existing racial prejudice of the South in general, and in Maycomb in particular. Scout does not understand that in terms of status, all Negroes are regarded as being lower even than the Ewells. This visit to church marks an important point in the children's education. For the first time they understand that Calpurnia leads a 'double life'. From her they learn the important lesson that you cannot change people against their will.

Text commentary

Chapter 13

Scout finds it difficult to talk to her aunt and dislikes certain aspects of her character. Notice how the children 'exchanged glances'. But there is a new maturity in Scout's attitude towards her aunt's stay.

It is soon obvious that **the author is mocking in her description of Aunt Alexandra.** Look at the section containing the words 'let any moral come along and she would uphold it'. What overall impression do you get of Aunt Alexandra? Aunt Alexandra seems quite disagreeable at first with her 'riverboat, boarding school manners'. She attempts to make Scout more lady-like, curbs the children's freedom and refuses to allow them to mix with the Cunninghams because the latter lack the right 'background'. She is at odds with Atticus about the way he is raising the children and thoroughly disagrees with his defending Tom Robinson. Scout never understands her aunt's preoccupation with 'family' and 'heredity' – with her references to what Scout amusingly calls 'other tribal groups'.

However, Aunt Alexandra mellows after the trial, when she sees what a strain the events are placing on her brother. Scout looks on her aunt with new respect when she sees her self-control at the missionary circle tea-party. Aunt Alexandra, in her turn, comes to regard Scout with more affection. She is particularly kind to Scout after Bob Ewell's attack.

Family characteristics are considered important in Maycomb, and no one clings more to this belief than Aunt Alexandra. She is particularly proud of the Finch family background and feels that Jem and Scout should also be made to feel proud of it. Atticus sees things differently. His discomfort is shown by the way he keeps saying: 'She asked me to tell you'. What other signs are there that

Atticus does not really share his sister's belief in living up to the family name? Scout and Jem are upset by the way Atticus is talking. In which way do they not want things to change?

Chapter 14

❝"What's rape?" I asked him...❞

No doubt remembering what he told his brother (at the end of Chapter 9), Atticus answers Scout's question truthfully, although using difficult legal terminology. Scout pretends to understand his definition and moves on to another query.

Scout's question about visiting Calpurnia shows us several things at once. Firstly, it shows how quick Aunt Alexandra is to impose her own views on her brother's household. This demonstrates the extent of her prejudice and intolerance. Secondly, it shows how quickly Scout responds to threats to Atticus's authority, emphasising Scout's youth and loyalty. Thirdly, it shows what a difficult position all this places Atticus in. He is not some superhuman figure who is able to be reasonable and fair because he is different from other people! His tolerance and lack of prejudice result in great strain. <u>Doing the right thing frequently involves making a sacrifice, and all real sacrifices hurt.</u>

Jem is beginning to understand things from an adult's point of view. He has some sense of the worry Atticus must be experiencing at the moment. Scout, who still sees the world very much as a child, has no idea that these undercurrents are present. Later, Jem is equally concerned that Dill should let his mother know where he is.

Look at the diplomatic way Atticus deals with Dill's unexpected arrival. He manages to be responsible, by informing Dill's aunt, without betraying the child's trust. The situation is managed by Atticus with humour and without anger.

Contrast Scout, who is sure of Atticus's and Jem's affection, with Dill, who has everything in the material sense but seems to be unwanted by his parents.

Chapter 15

<u>The use of the child's perspective by the narrator increases the tension in the story.</u> The reader understands the danger Atticus is in, but Scout does not.

For the most part, we never get to know the people in Maycomb who are Atticus's friends and who support his actions. This increases our sense of Atticus's isolation. Why might the author have wanted to do this?

❝ *As Atticus's fists went to his hips, so did Jem's...* **❞**

Explore

Look at Atticus's reaction after the men's cars have gone and compare it with Scout's question about whether or not they can now go home.

Why does Jem refuse to go home? He knows something about the present situation that Scout has failed to grasp. <u>It is only thanks to Scout innocently talking to Mr Cunningham about his son, that a crisis is averted.</u>

Chapter 16

<u>Scout realises what the true situation was the night before, and over a tense breakfast table views are aired regarding this and the possible violence that could have transpired.</u> Although Mr BB Underwood is prejudiced against Negroes he believes it is the job of the law, and not the mob, to

bring a person to justice. Hence his willingness to defend Atticus against attack. Mr BB Underwood, like Mrs Dubose, is a character who can be admired and condemned at the same time.

Notice the different attitudes that Atticus and Aunt Alexandra have towards Calpurnia. Atticus respects and values Calpurnia. He speaks frankly in front of her because he sees her as part of the family. To Aunt Alexandra, Calpurnia is just a Negro, and therefore to admit in front of her that a white person is prejudiced against Negroes is just adding to their grievances.

> **❝So it took an eight-year-old child to bring 'em to their senses, didn't it? ❞**

Explore

Look closely at the relationships between the characters in the film version. Do they reflect those in the novel?

Atticus's observation reflects a crucial theme of the book: it took a child, Scout, to remind the adult, Mr Cunningham, that he is still a human being. When he was made to remember that he is also a father and a friend, he saw the error of his behaviour. Remember what Miss Maudie said about Atticus being the same at home as he is in public.

How does Miss Maudie's attitude to the trial differ from that of the Maycomb population in general? What does it say about her sympathy for Tom Robinson and her sensitivity towards others? This episode highlights the way in which pressure from others can change a person's behaviour. Does the same thing happen at the trial?

Miss Crawford does not have the honesty to admit her true motives for going into town. Consider whether Miss Maudie's sarcasm is justified. Miss Crawford is quite the opposite of Miss Maudie. She embodies the worst aspects of Maycomb people. She is bigoted, prejudiced, unkind and a gossip. She filled the children with wild notions about Boo Radley. She teases Scout unkindly at Aunt Alexandra's tea party.

The depth of racial prejudice in Maycomb is emphasised in the account of Dolphus Raymond's life and the sad predicament of half-caste children. Given what we know already about the narrow and rigid views of the Southern whites, is Dolphus Raymond's exile from their community, even though voluntary, all that surprising?

> 66 *We knew there was a crowd, but we had not bargained for the multitudes in the first-floor doorway* 99

It is typical of the people of Maycomb County that they would cram the courtroom full to observe the circus within it. This is probably the most exciting thing to happen in Maycomb for years. Note that this is in keeping with the nature of a town where everyone minds each other's business. Remember the gossip about Boo Radley and popular town opinion.

Scout finds out that Atticus did not choose to defend Tom Robinson: he was appointed to do so. She is puzzled because, had she known this, it would have been a good excuse to use when people were taunting her. Why didn't Atticus mention this to the children? In what way does this make him a more courageous man? Re-read Atticus's conversation with his brother at the end of Chapter 9.

The narrator draws a very amusing picture of Judge Taylor, from the cleaning of his nails with his pocket knife, to the chewing and regurgitation of his cigars. Despite these habits, he is an astute and competent judge. He is another character whose nature is different from his appearance. The novel is full of such people: it is a central message of the book that people should not be judged by external appearance. A civilised society depends upon everybody learning to recognise this simple fact. The children's admission to the balcony underlines their lack of prejudice, but it also solves some problems for the author. Atticus would surely have sent them home if he could see them.

Chapter 17

Again the older Scout recalls incidents and observations from her youth that she did not understand at the time. She misinterprets Jem's sudden excitement because she does not understand the necessity for calling a doctor in a rape case. Jem does, and this contrast in the children's responses draws our attention to this revealing piece of testimony.

> *a little bantam cock of a man rose and strutted to the stand...*

The way Bob Ewell is described is deliberately intended to make the reader dislike this arrogant little man. The only way that Mr Ewell is 'better' than his Negro neighbour is in the colour of his skin. Notice the effect his crude language has on the public in court. Why is there such an uproar? And why would Mr Ewell be pleased with this result, do you think? Bob Ewell is a drunkard, almost certainly a cruel father, and a liar. He is a poor farmer but, unlike the Cunninghams, he does not try to live with dignity; instead he lives on relief cheques issued by the State. His children are filthy and half-starved because he spends his relief money on drink. He is often violent towards his children, and is trying here to turn one particular bout of violence to his advantage by accusing Tom Robinson of rape.

> *There has been a request that this courtroom be cleared of spectators...*

Once again, interest is heightened by the older Scout describing things that the younger Scout cannot understand, but that the reader can. Judge Taylor rules his court with order and common sense, and although the outcome of the trial is unjust, neither he nor the court is open to criticism. Both are fair. The fault lies with the prejudice of the people, particularly those sitting on the jury. As

Text commentary

Atticus says in his summing up (Chapter 20), <u>the law can only function properly if the people allow it to,</u> for 'a jury is only as sound as the men who make it up'. Scout wants to know why people like Miss Maudie never seem to get onto juries, because then she feels that justice would be done. <u>This reveals another type of prejudice – women were not allowed on juries at this time.</u>

The narrator describes Mr Ewell with great sarcasm. Why is it funny to call him a 'fragrant gardenia'? Scout refers to him as a 'red little rooster'. Why is this image appropriate? Scout's main concern is that Mr Ewell gains an advantage over Atticus by carrying the sympathy of the crowd. Emotional appeal seems to sway the crowd, not common sense. Mr Ewell is left-handed. This detail, together with another fact which we learn about Tom Robinson, is suddenly produced at this stage. Why would knowing these things earlier have spoiled the novel?

Chapter 18

❝ *Mayella looked as if she tried to keep clean...* ❞

Mayella has tried to rise above her squalid living conditions and, <u>in contrast to the rest of her family,</u> has some dignity. When her lies are exposed by Atticus, it is the fact that she has betrayed herself that hurts her so much. Mr Ewell also betrays himself but, because he has only the false dignity of the arrogant, he does not care – in fact, he glories in it.

Judge Taylor's approach to Mayella is sympathetic, even if he does find her hard to cope with. Mayella is quite a pathetic figure. She is so unused to being treated with routine courtesy that she feels that Atticus must be making fun of her when he calls her 'ma'am'. What vision must Mayella have of her own situation if she thinks that Atticus is making fun of her for having no friends?

Mayella's deceit brings Tom Robinson to trial. Although perhaps she cannot be forgiven for this vicious lie, both Atticus and Scout feel sympathy for her because they know she is the victim of her father's cruelty. Scout senses that she must be very lonely. It is perhaps understandable that she responded to Tom Robinson's kindness.

Mayella's position in white society is really summed up by Aunt Alexandra who describes the family as 'trash'. In Chapter 19 Scout reflects that Mayella ' was as sad… as what Jem called a mixed child: white people wouldn't have anything to do with her because she lived among pigs; Negroes wouldn't have anything to do with her because she was white.'

> **Somehow, Atticus had hit her hard in a way that was not clear to me…**

Why is Atticus not triumphant at casting doubt on Mayella's testimony? Knowing his ability to put himself in other people's shoes, what do you think is Atticus's opinion of her? Is Atticus's reaction here similar to his reaction when he was obliged to shoot the mad dog? It seems that only a bully would deliberately hurt someone so entirely less fortunate than they are.

Chapter 19

> **Tom, did you rape Mayella Ewell?**

The predicament that Tom found himself in when Bob Ewell saw him with Mayella sums up the position of the Negro in the prejudiced South. Whichever way he acted in this difficult situation, he would have seemed guilty in the eyes of white people. If he tried to defend himself against a white woman's advances the situation would be seen to be of his making, and therefore his fault. If he ran, as he did, it would be taken as an admission of guilt. <u>He was in an impossible position.</u>

Explore

As a revision technique you could draw a spidergram of the trial that clearly demonstrates what is said during each person's testimony. It is vital to have a clear understanding of the trial.

Despite his casual manner, Judge Taylor is strict about the correct procedure. Link Deas speaks out of turn, therefore he has to be called to order. Look at how Atticus reacts to the judge's outburst – he understands that there is a certain amount of acting in the judge's performance.

The inferiority of the Negro's position in the South is again underlined here by Mr Gilmer's outrage at the insulting suggestion that a black man could show sympathy for a white woman. The majority of whites see this as gross impertinence. Why should this be so?

> *This was as much as I heard of Mr Gilmer's cross-examination...*

There is a big difference in the sensitivity of Dill and Scout. Dill is disturbed by Mr Gilmer's tone and begins to cry. Scout's attitude can partly be explained by her greater 'experience' of court matters (she expects the prosecuting lawyer to be harsh). Nevertheless it is Dill, not Scout, who grasps the reality of the awful position that Tom Robinson is in.

Chapter 20

Scout has accepted the stories about Mr Raymond and so she judges him at first by his reputation. Her opinion changes as she talks to him.

What do you think of Mr Raymond's behaviour? Is he merely feeding people's prejudice by pretending to be odd? Would he do

Explore

Relate this to what is thought of Boo Radley and Tom Robinson. Also remember the way Francis quoted his elders' opinions to Scout about Atticus.

better to set both Blacks and Whites a good example by showing that 'normal' people can live in racial harmony?

Mr Raymond reveals his secret to the children because he respects their innocence. They might understand him because they have not yet been contaminated by prejudice. Like Atticus, Mr Raymond represents the tolerant Southerner. He can see the 'hell white people give coloured folks'. He is not blinded by fear and hatred.

Jem, who has followed the trial with understanding, is confident that Atticus will win. But he is basing his judgement only upon what has gone on in the courtroom – on the evidence which has been presented. Atticus knows that the jury's verdict will be based more upon what they brought into the courtroom with them – their preconceived attitudes, opinions, and their prejudice.

> **❝**Atticus paused, then he did something I never saw him do before or since...**❞**

Scout's humorous remarks about Atticus's state of dress indicate the exceptional nature of this case. Atticus is making great efforts to convince the jury not only that Tom is innocent, but that they must defy their ingrained prejudice, and stand up for a black man against a white. Notice the tone of voice and the manner that Atticus adopts to accomplish this.

Explore

See if you can highlight the persuasion techniques that Atticus uses in his defence of Tom. Would that speech have persuaded you?

Atticus sums up the crux of the trial. The time-honoured, rigid code of behaviour has been broken, and broken by a white person. Atticus is trying to make the jury face this. They must have the courage to question their long-held beliefs. They must accept that the real world is not the way they have come to see it. <u>Atticus tries to show that all people are equal in law.</u>

Chapter 21

> **Mister Jem, don't you know any better'n to take your little sister to that trial?**

This is another example of humour arising from Scout's innocence: she has no idea why Calpurnia thinks the trial is unsuitable for her, but is delighted that it is Jem who is getting into trouble for a change.

Explore

Do you think, judging from Reverend Skye's reaction, that he or anyone else in the negro community believes that Tom Robinson will be acquitted?

The final comment about Judge Taylor's performance comes from a Negro. Reverend Sykes says that, 'he was mighty fair-minded', even leaning towards their side a little. In this way, it is emphasised that the law itself is not wrong, but people's interpretation of law sometimes is. The way people view justice is influenced a great deal by their prejudices.

Jem is convinced that the evidence is clear-cut, and confident that the verdict will reflect this. His growing-up process is far from complete; he has still to learn about the complexities of human nature and their effect on human behaviour.

With its verdict, the jury has killed the 'mockingbird', which is here a symbol not only of a gentle, harmless creature like Tom, but also of human values and justice itself. The jury does not value these fragile things.

The recalling of the mad dog incident says something about Atticus and the courage he has to summon up at this point. Why will Atticus need to be brave? Who does he have to face? What knowledge does he have to accept? (Bear in mind the consolation which Miss Maudie offers the children in the middle of Chapter 22.)

Explore

Note the degree of respect that the Negroes show Atticus, despite his losing the trial.

Text commentary

Quick quiz 3

Uncover the plot

Delete two of the three alternatives given, to find the correct plot. Beware possible misconceptions and muddles.

Jem and Scout go to court/church/jail with Calpurnia. A collection is taken up for Helen/Mayella/Lula, Tom Robinson's wife, because she can no longer find work. On their return they find out that Aunt Alexandra has come to live with them: her presence in the house, and Jem's new-found aggression/education/maturity, make life uncomfortable/pleasant/unbearable for Scout. Dill runs away from Aunt Rachel/home/an animal show.

Tom Robinson is moved to the Maycomb jail: a group of men, led by Heck Tate/Joshua St Clair/Walter Cunningham, tries to 'get at' him but the tense situation is resolved when Scout/Jem/Dill innocently intervenes. The trial begins and Jem, Scout and Dill watch from the Negroes' balcony/cubby-hole/porch. Mayella Ewell and her father accuse Tom of having beaten Mayella and then raped her, hurting her badly on the left side/the right side/both sides of her face: Atticus makes it plain that the Negro, crippled in his left/his right/both arm(s), could not have inflicted the injuries, and suggests that her father beat her. Tom, Atticus's only/second/third witness, claims that Mayella attempted to beat/patronise/seduce him. Calpurnia fetches the children home, but they return for the verdict: guilty. As Atticus/Mr Gilmer/Judge Taylor leaves the court-room, all the Negroes stand as a gesture of respect.

Who? What? Why? When? Where? How?

1   Who is 'growin' up'?

2   Why won't people employ Helen Robinson?

3   How does Calpurnia speak in church? What explanation does she give?

4   With what is Aunt Alexandra preoccupied?

5   What does Aunt Alexandra try to persuade Atticus to do, and why?

6   How does Jem break their childhood code?

7   Why has Dill run away, and how does his home life compare with Scout's?

8   What is Atticus's 'dangerous question', and why is it dangerous?

9   Why is Scout's intervention at the jail more effective than Jem's?

10   What makes Dill cry?

Chapters 22 to 31

Chapter 22

Atticus does not try to conceal from Jem that, in life, the just and right thing is not always done. Jem is devastated, but Atticus realises that he has got to learn the harsh realities of life. **Atticus acknowledges that only children seem to have been moved by the injustice of the case.** The adults' view is that there is nothing anyone can do to change matters. Is it attitudes like this that prevent things from changing?

"Miss Stephanie's nose quivered with curiosity"

Notice the contrast in attitude between Miss Crawford and Miss Maudie. Miss Crawford disapproves of the children being in court, especially on the Coloured balcony. Miss Maudie treats the children no differently, and even bakes them cakes as a treat.

Contrast Miss Maudie's view of religion with that of the strict Baptists earlier in the book. To Miss Maudie, Christianity is about loving one's neighbour and treating people equally. She understands that at certain times in life a Christian is called upon to live up to these beliefs. She tries to give hope to Jem, by saying that there are good men in Maycomb who try to be true Christians. She also makes an interesting point about Judge Taylor. **He deliberately appointed Atticus because he knew that Atticus would give Maycomb the best chance of seeing justice done.** Do you think that real progress has been made, and that Aunt Maudie's optimism is justified?

Explore

Do you think there is potential for attitudes to change in Maycomb?

Like Atticus, Miss Maudie is a realist and did not expect Atticus to win the case. But she sees signs for optimism in that at least he made the jury think for a long time. Because of his youth, Jem cannot accept this; he does not realise that ingrained attitudes and behaviour cannot be changed overnight.

66 *I think I'll be a clown when I get grown...* 99

This is Dill's reaction to the injustice of the verdict. He is utterly disillusioned with people; he wants to separate himself from them and become a clown who laughs at them. Who else has made him feel disillusioned with people?

Chapter 23

66 *According to Miss Stephanie Crawford, however, ...* 99

Atticus reacts calmly to Mr Ewell's assault. The children are naturally worried for their father's safety, because they believe Mr Ewell's threats. Atticus's hatred of violence makes him refuse to use a gun. He tries to make the children look at the situation from Mr Ewell's point of view. He is being extraordinarily reasonable in saying he would rather Mr Ewell vent his anger on him than on Mayella. Why might Mr Ewell be angry with Mayella? Do future events prove Atticus right, or is his faith in the basic goodness of all men too great? For once, Aunt Alexandra's interpretation of human nature is more accurate than Atticus's

66 *We ought to do away with juries...* 99

Jem has still to grasp the complexities of adult life. Atticus explains the flaws in the legal system, but Jem demands a simple, easy solution to them. He does not appreciate that laws can only be changed when enough people want them changed. Atticus warns Jem that <u>things</u> <u>do</u> <u>not</u> <u>happen</u> <u>overnight</u>. This echoes something Calpurnia said earlier when she was talking about the level of general education among black people, and their resistance to learning.

Notice Aunt Alexandra's rigid views on 'background' again. The Cunninghams are not suitable for the Finches to associate with because of their inferior background; Aunt Alexandra calls them

'trash'. (Contrast with Atticus's definition of trash in Chapter 27). Is Aunt Alexandra influenced more by social position or by personal qualities in her judgement of others?

In the depressing context of racial prejudice and social snobbery, the relationship between Jem and Scout makes a cheerful contrast. Scout is eager to say the right thing to please her brother, while he, developing a sense of maturity, tries to give her advice and consolation. Jem's amusing pride in the new hair on his chest shows that he is still a child at heart, while Scout's wry comment that it looks lovely (when in fact she can't see anything) is just as touching.

Explore

Which side of the debate do you agree with? Which side do you feel that Atticus would support?

Jem's attempt to explain people's behaviour by splitting them into four categories is criticised by Scout. She recognises the worth of people like the Cunninghams and explains their difference as merely the result of a lack of education. Jem believes that she is idealistic in thinking there is only one kind of people, and thinks she will eventually become disillusioned, like him.

Chapter 24

> ❝*I didn't know whether to go into the dining-room or stay out...*❞

There is a new maturity in Scout. <u>She is learning to be considerate and put other people's feelings before her own.</u> She is careful to keep her dress clean in order to spare Calpurnia work. She also sits with the ladies, even though such gatherings fill her with 'vague apprehension'. Scout does this purely because she senses that if she does so her aunt will be pleased. Later in the chapter her admiration for her aunt increases as she shows her self-control.

Text commentary

Scout realises that growing up takes a long time. She is embarrassed by her own frankness in revealing that she is still wearing her trousers under her dress! Miss Maudie, loyal to Scout, does not join in the laughter. But Miss Crawford shows her unkind nature by trying to get a laugh at Scout's expense by referring to the children's presence at Tom's trial.

The Maycomb ladies do not see their own hypocrisy, perhaps because it is easier to feel kinder towards people who are far away. They expect the Negroes to forget about Tom Robinson and get on with their lives as usual. They are not prepared to allow black people any status at all, let alone equal status with themselves.

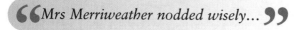

❝*Mrs Merriweather nodded wisely...* ❞

Explore

Can you make sense of the Maycomb ladies' sympathy for poor Africans when you consider their callous disregard for the Negroes in their own midst?

Although Scout does not understand who the ladies are referring to here, it is obvious to the reader that they mean Atticus. Far from appreciating that he was trying to ensure that Tom received justice, they interpret his actions as merely 'stirring up' the Negroes, and making them dissatisfied. Miss Maudie is angry with their criticism of Atticus and a moment of tension occurs in the room.

It is interesting to note the change in Aunt Alexandra. Her love for her brother and the knowledge of what it has cost him emotionally to go through with this case has separated her from the views and attitudes she would normally have shared with the other Maycomb ladies. Hence her gratitude to Miss Maudie for standing up for Atticus. She diverts the ladies from their topic of conversation by handing out the refreshments.

Although Scout has not fully understood the ladies' veiled comments about her father and the Negroes, she concludes that she prefers the frankness of male company to the hypocritical talk of the ladies.

Text commentary

66 *Tom's dead.* 99

Notice the effect the news of Tom's death has on Aunt Alexandra. Her concern for her brother has brought her to see the situation from his point of view, and she is very moved.

Maybe she realises that '__background__' – as Miss Maudie points out – __is not merely a matter of coming from a 'good' family, but is more a matter of having the courage to try to do what is right, even if it flies in the face of social custom.__

Miss Maudie's definition does of course allow that it would be possible for a black family to have 'background', whereas Aunt Alexandra's definition would never allow such a possibility.

Text commentary

Chapter 25

We see again the idea behind the mockingbird symbol; that it is wrong to kill creatures that do no harm. Jem prevents Scout from killing insects because, 'they don't bother you'. When Tom Robinson's wife is told of his death, she falls to the ground 'like a giant with a big foot just came along and stepped on her'. If white society is the giant, how accurate is this image?

66 *Maycomb was interested by the news of Tom's death for perhaps two days...* 99

Note how the people of Maycomb receive the news of Tom's death. The repetition of the word 'typical' demonstrates how easily they slot the death into their preconceived ideas about Negroes. As with the alleged rape, Tom's behaviour is interpreted to his disadvantage – no matter what he does, in their eyes he has no human dignity.

Explore

Look on the internet at Monroeville, where Harper Lee grew up, to see what Maycomb would have been like.

Notice the cynicism of the Maycomb people. They are unmoved by BB Underwood's impassioned editorial. They see it as a ploy to get Mr Underwood's work published in a more prestigious paper! The image of the mockingbird is repeated in the editorial and underlines the wickedness of killing innocent creatures.

Scout finally wakes up to the truth about the trial of Tom Robinson. Until now she has taken the events of the trial at face value and has been puzzled by the reactions of Jem and Dill. Now she understands why the whole affair is such a tragedy.

Chapter 26

Although Scout is beginning to mature, it does not mean she understands or behaves entirely like an adult yet. She cannot understand the decision of the people of Maycomb, who have voted to re-elect Atticus to the state legislature, so she accepts the mystery without trying to unravel it. Atticus's re-election is a sign that Miss Maudie's optimism for the future is not altogether without cause.

<u>Scout becomes increasingly aware of people's basic hypocrisy in thinking about the world.</u> We've seen how uncomfortable she felt in the company of the missionary ladies who pitied the African tribe of Mrunas. Now she is faced with the strange contrast between those who condemn the persecution of the Jews but do not condemn the treatment to which the Negroes in their own town are subjected.

Text commentary

Explore

Do you feel that Atticus has come to terms with this knowledge?

Jem still has not been able to come to terms with the knowledge that people are not as good as he once imagined.

Chapter 27

❝Aunt Alexandra was thriving...❞

The narrator gently satirises the attitudes of the Maycomb ladies. 'They had so little sense of family that the whole tribe was one big family' mocks the exaggerated importance that Maycomb people attach to family names. Would everybody in the South have been better off if, like the Mrunas, they could see themselves as belonging to 'one big family'?

❝Maycomb was itself again...❞

The National Recovery Act was introduced by President Roosevelt, but was seen not to be helping the country to recover from the economic depression. It was therefore cancelled (repealed) by the Supreme Court.

<u>The author's scene-setting and cautious tone create suspense.</u>
Atticus and Aunt Alexandra have decided not to go to the pageant, so the children will return home alone. Aunt Alexandra has a feeling something might happen.

Chapter 28

❝Jem was becoming almost as good as Atticus at making you feel right when things went wrong...❞

Jem is becoming tactful and diplomatic. He is rivalling his father in his ability to say the right thing at the right moment.

Scout is not particularly curious about the stranger on their porch. Of course, she does not yet know that it is Boo Radley. Her lack of interest is ironic, because for the last two years she has been anxious to see him.

Chapter 29

> **❝For once in his life, Atticus's instinctive courtesy failed him...❞**

Explore

This is the second time that Atticus has misjudged a potentially life-threatening situation. Remember the other was the lynch mob.

A strong note of sympathy for Atticus is struck here. The attack on his children has affected him deeply, and now he has to endure the shock of Bob Ewell's death. Whom does he think has killed him? For one so wise, **Atticus made a great error in judgement over Bob Ewell.** He miscalculated the lengths to which Bob Ewell would go in search of his revenge. His faith in people has, in a sense, let him down.

Look at the description of Boo Radley. Although he is as pale as a ghost, he does not have any of the frightening characteristics with which the children once furnished him. He is not a rampaging monster of the night; in fact, he is very shy.

Chapter 30

> **❝I don't want him growing up with a whisper about him❞**

Atticus believes that Jem killed Bob Ewell, but he wants there to be no cover-up. He wants the facts dealt with fairly in a court of law. Again he has made another serious error of judgement. As Heck Tate points out later, with his injured arm and his lack of weight Jem could not possibly have stabbed Bob Ewell. **This is the second** time that an injured arm has been used to show that someone could not have committed a crime against a member of the Ewell family.

Heck Tate is trying to protect Boo Radley as to highlight what he did would put an end to the quiet life he chooses to lead.

❝Atticus sat looking at the floor for a long time❞

Scout understands the sheriff. She likens Boo Radley – an innocent figure who has only done good – to a mockingbird who does no harm but merely sings. **The two strands of the story are linked within this one image**, because Tom Robinson was also likened to a mockingbird.

Chapter 31

❝He gently released my hand, opened the door and went inside … I never saw him again❞

Notice how much Scout has grown up. She is ceasing to be the child who sees everything from a selfish point of view. She finally has taken Atticus's lesson to heart; as she comments: **'you never really know a man until you stand in his shoes and walk around in them'.**

Quick quiz 4

Uncover the plot

Delete two of the three alternatives given, to find the correct plot. Beware possible misconceptions and muddles.

The Negroes show their displeasure at/appreciation of/ignorance of what Atticus has tried to do by spitting at him/cursing him/sending him presents of food, but the humiliated Tom Robinson/Mayella Ewell/Bob Ewell spits at him and threatens him publicly. An appeal against/for/before Tom's conviction is planned, but Atticus arrives in the middle of one of Aunt Alexandra's missionary teas with the news that Tom has escaped/been lynched/been shot dead trying to escape from jail. Life in Maycomb seems to settle down, although after Bob Ewell finds and loses a job, Judge Taylor/Johnson/Gilmer is disturbed by a nocturnal visitor and Tom's wife Helen is persecuted by the Ewell family. Returning at night from a Halloween pageant, Jem and Scout are attacked. Bob Ewell/Cecil Jacobs/Boo Radley is discovered dead at the scene, and it is revealed that his killer was Jem/Boo Radley/ Scout's costume, come to defend the children. The Sheriff persuades/fails to persuade/begs Atticus to pretend that Ewell fell on his knife, to save Boo from conviction/public anger/public attention.

Who? What? Why? When? Where? How?

1   *What is Atticus's reaction to the Negroes' generosity?*

2   *Why does Miss Maudie give Jem a piece from the big cake?*

3   *Why do you think Judge Taylor named Atticus to defend Tom?*

4   *Who took 'considerable wearing down' before pronouncing Tom guilty? Why was this surprising?*

5   *When Miss Maudie says, 'His food doesn't stick going down, does it?' to whom is she referring?*

6   *What is Maycomb's reaction to Tom's death?*

7   *Despite the verdict, Bob Ewell still harbours a grudge. Why?*

8   *What made the 'shiny clean line' on Scout's costume?*

9   *Why is Boo's skin so white?*

10   *What does Mr Tate mean when he says Atticus has been unable to 'put two and two together' for once?*

Who says?

1   Who says: 'If there's just one kind of folks, why can't they get along'?

2   Who says: 'Don't you look at me, Link Deas, like I was dirt'?

3   Who says: 'Because – he – is – trash, that's why you can't play with him'?

4   Who says: 'Good Lord... You're still standing'?

5   Who says: 'Well, it'd be sort of like shootin' a mockingbird, wouldn't it?'

To kill a mockingbird

1   Who do you think is the 'mockingbird' of the story? Why?

2   Why does Scout say to Atticus that letting people know the truth about Bob Ewell's death would be like 'shootin' a mockingbird'?

3   What do her words tell you about Scout?

4   Which characters do you think would 'kill a mockingbird'? (In some cases this may be clear-cut; others may be more difficult.)

Writing essays on *To Kill A Mockingbird*

- Read the questions very carefully, identifying all the **key words** in the question, e.g. **compare**, **contrast**, **explore**. It is very unlikely that simple retelling of the story will gain you much credit.

- Jot down a list of main points. Make an essay plan (see page 74) which shows what you are going to write about in each paragraph. Make sure that you have a clear way of linking paragraphs. Refer back to the original question to ensure that you don't digress.

- Try to **summarise** your response to the question so the examiner has some idea of how you plan to approach it. Then **jump straight into your argument**. As you write your essay, refer back to your list of points/essay plan.

- Answer **all** of the question and make sure you attempt all of the questions on the examination. Marks can always be gained most easily at the start of an answer.

- Take care with presentation, spelling, punctuation and grammar. It is unwise to use slang or abbreviations. Always write in paragraphs, starting a new line and indenting quotations of more than a few words.

- Use quotation or paraphrase when it is relevant and contributes to the quality and clarity of your answer.

- It is most important to always back up what you say. Remember: **point–quotation–comment**. This will ensure that the essay remains analytical.

- Use your conclusion to sum up all your points and relate them back to the original question.

- Finally, leave yourself with five minutes to **proofread** your work, to check for and correct any mistakes.

You may need to write a coursework essay and could use the novel as the twentieth-century comparison for a Wider Reading assignment.

- There must be a specific ground for comparison. Many pre-twentieth-century novels supply examples of small-town prejudice. *To Kill A Mockingbird* offers a more lethal presentation of this narrow-mindedness.

- When writing a coursework essay it is **essential** to refer to the **historical, social and cultural background** of the text. The background of old Southern attitudes is a key part of your essay.

- You should develop an argument throughout and not give way to storytelling. Make an essay plan and stick to it. This will ensure that your work remains focused on the question. If you are writing a comparative piece, the comparison should be made throughout the essay.

- You are able to draft your response before completing the neat copy. You should take advantage of this to ensure that your final piece is as polished as possible.

- As with examination questions, make sure your conclusion summarises your arguments, and it is only at this stage that you should consider offering your own opinion. Until the conclusion you should avoid using personal pronouns and simply present your arguments supported by evidence from the text. Again, proofread to check for mistakes.

- Many essays will be longer than 1,000 words, but by how much depends on the essay title and the advice of your teacher.

Writing essays

Key quotations

The following section demonstrates how to effectively use quotations within an essay to evidence your argument (point – quotation – comment).

Mrs Dubose is courageous because she knows she is dying but decides she must free herself from her morphine addiction first. After she dies, Atticus explains to the children:

> *I wanted you to see what real courage is, instead of getting the idea that courage is a man with a gun in his hand. It's when you know you're licked before you begin but you begin anyway and you see it through no matter what* (Chapter 10)

The type of **courage** Atticus describes could just as easily refer to his defending Tom Robinson. The outcome of the trial is a foregone conclusion, but Atticus sees it through anyway.

The Ewell **family** are seen by the townspeople as 'white trash' and have been for generations.

> *Atticus said the Ewells had been the disgrace of Maycomb for three generations. None of them had done an honest day's work in his recollection* (Chapter 3)

The Ewell children are neglected and, for their sake, the townspeople make allowances about the family's behaviour.

Atticus explains one of the reasons that Mayella accused Tom Robinson of rape:

66 *She was white, and she tempted a Negro. She did something that, in our society, is unspeakable: she kissed a black man* **99** (Chapter 19)

This clearly shows how **prejudiced** society in the novel is towards the black community.

Atticus explains the current racial **prejudice** against black people:

66 *In our courts, when it's a white man's word against a black man's, the white man always wins. They're ugly, but these are the facts of life* **99** (Chapter 23)

This shows how such a miscarriage of justice is allowed to take place among normally rational people.

Scout understands that Boo Bradley should not be exposed as Bob Ewell's killer as he lives a solitary and private life. She explains:

66 *Mr Tate was right…Well it'd be sort of like shootin' a mockingbird, wouldn't it?* **99** (Chapter 30)

Scout shows that she has learnt from Atticus, and that Boo should be saved from becoming another 'victim' of the town.

Key quotations

Exam questions

1. To what extent was Tom Robinson's fate sealed the moment Mayella Ewell accused him of rape?

2. How does the reader's view of Boo Radley change throughout the novel?

3. Compare different portrayals of courage in To Kill A Mockingbird.

4. How do the characters of Scout and Jem change and grow up during the course of the novel?

5. In what ways do the opinions of Atticus and Miss Maudie Atkinson differ from those of the majority of the residents of Maycomb county?

6. Atticus tells Jem 'it's a sin to kill a mockingbird'. How does Harper Lee convey her views on the treatment of 'mockingbirds' through the characters of Tom Robinson and Boo Radley?

7. Examine the importance of family in To Kill A Mockingbird.

8. Atticus considers that it is incredible that the jury took a few hours to convict Tom Robinson. Explain the significance of this achievement in small-town America in the 1930s.

9. Atticus tells Scout that you don't really know a man 'until you stand in his shoes and walk around in them'. What has Scout learnt about life from other people's perspectives by the end of the novel?

10. The trial of Tom Robinson is a clear example of racial prejudice at work. Analyse the forms of prejudice that are encountered in the novel and explore the ways in which Harper Lee makes clear her own views on the matter.

11. Despite its serious themes, To Kill A Mockingbird contains much humour. Give an account of various types of humour and suggest why you think Harper Lee included it.

12 Compare and contrast the attitudes towards the trial of the adults in the town of Maycomb and the children. Is there any major difference in their attitudes to the outcome of the trial?

13 Explore the ways in which Harper Lee uses her narrative structure to convey the childish views of the young Scout and to show the benefits of hindsight through the adult perspective.

14 To what extent is Jem right to feel disillusioned by society at the end of the novel?

15 It has been suggested that Mayella Ewell is just as much a victim as Boo Radley and Tom Robinson. With close reference to text explore whether this is a valid argument.

16 With detailed reference to text, explore the ways in which Harper Lee gives the reader an insight into the black community through the character of Calpurnia.

17 How does the use of the first person narrative in To Kill A Mockingbird shape the reader's changing attitudes to Boo Radley?

18 In what ways does the relationship between Jem, Scout and Atticus change and develop throughout the course of the novel?

19 How does the reader's view on justice change throughout the novel? Could the novel be seen to be disillusioning?

20 Discuss to what extent the character of Mayella Ewell is a victim, for whom the reader should feel sympathy, and to what extent she is the persecutor of an innocent man.

21 To what extent could Atticus be said to be an "ideal father" and "upstanding pillar of the community" in To Kill A Mockingbird?

Spidergrams for questions 1, 3 and 11 are shown on pages 75–77.

There are several ways of planning an essay either for coursework or as part of an examination. One of the quickest, easiest and most simple to construct and follow is the spidergram. Creating a spidergram is easy, just complete the following steps.

- Put the key words of the essay question in the centre your spidergram and work outwards from this.

- Make sure you use different colours if the essay asks you to look at either different characters or different themes. This will make them easy to isolate at a glance.

- Draw lines out from the centre that relate directly to the question. From these lines, draw further lines and write anything specifically related to this area of the question.

- Remember, only have one idea at the end of each line or your drawing may become confusing.

- The next few pages show how you could use spidergrams to plan the answers to three of the sample essay questions.

- If you find that using spidergrams is not for you, don't panic, there are other ways of planning your answers.

- You can underline the keywords in the title to ensure that you understand the focus of the essay. Then write down in bullet points what you will write in each paragraph, from the introduction to the conclusion.

- When you have done this, try to find a relevant quotation to support each of your points and either jot down the quotation or, if it is more than a few words, the page reference. This is so that you will be able to find it quickly when you come to write your essay.

- Make sure that you stick to your plan, and keep referring back to the question in order to avoid digressing from it.

- In an examination, always hand in your plan as you may get some credit for it if you do not quite finish the question.

Compare different portrayals of courage in *To Kill A Mockingbird*

Different types of courage (central node)

Personal
- Scout being mocked for not fighting back when her father is called a 'nigger lover'
  - Has to rise above being called a coward
  - Asked not to fight by Atticus
  - Also catches his trousers on the fence

Doomed to failure
- Mrs Dubose curing herself of her morphine addiction before dying (would die anyway)
  - Did this because she wanted to die 'free as a bird' (succeeded)
  - She did not need to as she had a right to die without pain
- Atticus defending Tom Robinson
  - White woman's word bound to be believed over that of a black man
  - Trial just a formality as demonstrated by views of the lynch mob

Physical
- Atticus shooting the mad dog terrorising the neighbourhood
  - Used to be known as 'One Shot Finch'
  - Doesn't want the children thinking courage is 'a man with a gun in his hand'

No courage
- Bob Ewell attacks Atticus at night through his children
  - Threatens people associated with the trial
  - Coward who attacks children
  - Beats his own daughter

Child's
- Jem running up and touching the Radley house
  - Proves his bravery to Scout and Dill

Selfless
- Killing Bob Ewell to stop him killing the children
- Boo Radley saving Scout and Jem from Bob Ewell
  - Carrying an injured Jem home, thus being seen

Spidergrams essay plans

Despite its serious themes, *To Kill A Mockingbird* contains much humour. Give an account of the various types of humour and suggest why you think Harper Lee included it.

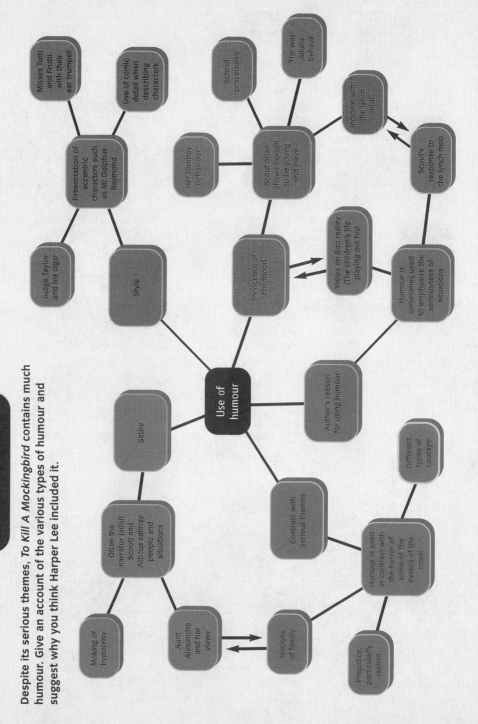

To what extent was Tom Robinson's fate sealed the moment Mayella Ewell accused him of rape?

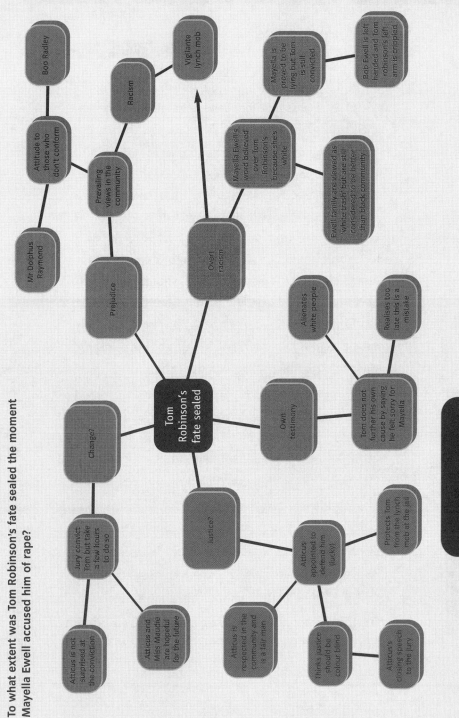

Central node: **Tom Robinson's fate sealed**

Prejudice
- Racism
  - Boo Radley
  - Attitude to those who don't conform
    - Mr Dolphus Raymond
  - Prevailing views in the community
  - Vigilante lynch mob

Overt racism
- Mayella Ewell's word believed over Tom Robinson's because she's white
  - Mayella is proved to be lying but Tom is still convicted
    - Bob Ewell is left handed and Tom Robinson's left arm is crippled
- Ewell family are viewed as 'white trash' but are still considered to be better than black community

Own testimony
- Tom does not further his own cause by saying he felt sorry for Mayella
  - Alienates white people
  - Realises too late this is a mistake

Change?
- Jury convict Tom but take a few hours to do so
  - Atticus is not surprised at the conviction
  - Atticus and Miss Maudie are hopeful for the future

Justice?
- Atticus appointed to defend him (lucky)
  - Atticus is respected in the community and is a fair man
  - Thinks justice should be colour blind
    - Atticus's closing speech to the jury
  - Protects Tom from the lynch mob at the jail

Sample response

To what extent was Tom Robinson's fate sealed the moment Mayella Ewell accused him of rape?

Tom Robinson's fate was decided the moment Mayella Ewell accused him of rape because he was a black man living in the American South in the 1930s. ✔ He was surrounded by a white racist community that had been brought up to believe that a white man's word meant more than a black man's. However, he stood slightly more of a chance when Judge Taylor appointed Atticus Finch to defend him because Atticus believed that justice should not depend on your colour. ✔ Atticus did everything in his power to make the jury realise that Tom was innocent and it was only his colour that made them doubt this. Sadly, he was unable to stop Tom from being falsely convicted of rape. ✔

Atticus clearly showed the jury that Tom Robinson was crippled and that under no circumstances would it have been possible for him to have hit or raped Mayella Ewell while holding her down. If he had been a white man Tom would have almost certainly been acquitted. It was racial prejudice that meant that Tom was found guilty. ✔

As Atticus said, 'This case is as simple as black and white', meaning that because Mayella is a white woman accusing a black man, her story is more likely to be believed than Tom Robinson's. Even a 'white trash' family like the Ewells, who are looked down on by the rest of the town are believed over a black man. ✔

It is clear that Tom Robinson did not commit the crime and that it was Mayella's drunken, abusive father who beat her so badly. ✔

Atticus conveys how dreadful Mayella's life is to the jury and how Bob Ewell is a drunk and a wastrel who leaves the children to fend for themselves. He shows how lonely she is and how unused she is to being treated with any respect. ✓ She becomes offended and thinks Atticus is mocking her when he calls her 'Miss Mayella'. Mayella knows that Atticus realises that she is lying and finds it very difficult to give evidence that does not suggest Tom Robinson's innocence. At the end of her testimony she shouts at Atticus and then bursts into tears. The narrator comments, 'Atticus had hit her hard in a way that was not clear to me, but it gave him no pleasure to do so.' ✓

Mayella knows she has lied and that now, thanks to Atticus, the jury and onlookers do too. She is frightened of her father and has been shamed before the entire court. Atticus feels sorry for her situation but is trying to prove her to be a liar to prove his client's innocence. ✓

It becomes clear that Tom Robinson had agreed to 'bust up a chiffarobe' for Mayella and, lonely and longing for companionship, she had thrown herself at him. ✓ When her father saw this he beat her and then forced her to accuse Tom Robinson of rape both to cover up his violence and to make up for her behaviour. The moment Tom Robinson was accused he was seen to be guilty and the trial was merely a formality. ✓

The 'final nail in Tom Robinson's coffin' was when he admitted to feeling sorry for Mayella Ewell. ✓ This was an unfortunate mistake as the people of Maycomb did not respond well to a black man feeling sorry for a white woman. It is possible to see the people's reaction through the prosecution lawyer Mr Gilmer's words: 'You felt sorry for her, you felt sorry for her?' Mr Gilmer is utterly astonished and allows Tom's comment to sink into the jury's minds. The white community did not like this comment, which further alienated Tom Robinson. ✓

Ultimately it is clear that Tom Robinson's fate was sealed the moment Mayella Ewell accused him of rape because he was a black man living in a racist community in 1930s Alabama. ✓ It is extremely unlikely that he would have won even if he had not admitted to feeling sorry for a white girl. ✓ Atticus tried extremely hard to win the case although all the odds were against him. The only positive thing that came out of the entire situation was that the jury took a few hours to come to this decision. ✓

Examiner's comments

This essay shows a clear understanding of what happened to Tom Robinson. It could have been improved by showing a more detailed understanding of the racial prejudice in the American South at this time. Answering the whole question in the first sentence should be avoided. Also, the candidate does not refer to the town's judgmental attitudes towards both black people and anyone else who does not conform – the racism should be seen as one aspect of the whole situation. The candidate could have commented on why the fact that the jury took time to come to its decision was a good sign.

Sample responses

Sample response

To what extent was Tom Robinson's fate sealed the moment Mayella Ewell accused him of rape?

Maycomb is presented as a town filled with many prejudices. ✓ However, in the American South of the 1930s racial prejudice was probably the most dangerous and potentially lethal. This can be seen in the case of Tom Robinson, a black man who is accused of raping a white woman. The implications of being found guilty of such a crime would almost certainly have been the enforcement of the death penalty. ✓ The likelihood of being found innocent would have been extremely remote, as can be seen through the trial of Tom Robinson. ✓

The only remotely positive aspect to Tom Robinson's trial is that Judge Taylor appoints Atticus Finch as his lawyer. ✓ Atticus is a dedicated defence lawyer who really cares about the law being without prejudice. ✓ In his closing speech at the trial he says: 'Our courts have their faults, as does any human institution, but in this country our courts are great levellers, and in our courts all men are created equal.' He makes this statement in the vain hope that the jury might be persuaded to see past Tom Robinson's colour and be judged purely in the eyes of the law. ✓ Sadly, in Maycomb at this time, this was never going to happen. ✓

Throughout the course of the trial it becomes increasingly evident that it would have been physically impossible for Tom Robinson to have committed the crime of which he is accused. ✓ The deformity of his left arm, stemming from a childhood accident, would have prevented this from being possible. ✓

Although all the evidence suggests Tom Robinson's innocence, it becomes increasingly apparent that the trial is merely a formality and that the white male jury had found him guilty before he entered the courtroom. ✓ This can be seen by the way in which the white men in the town form a lynch mob and head to the Maycomb jail prior to the trial with the intention of dispensing their own form of vigilante justice. ✓ They make their intentions clear to Atticus, who sits outside the jail guarding Tom, and do not hide the fact that if Atticus does not let them through then he too is at risk: 'You know what we want ... Get aside from the door, Mr Finch.' The mob becomes more aggressive ✓ until it is only Scout talking to one of them about his son that brings him to his senses and makes him a rational human being once more. It is here that it becomes clear that opinions may change but that it will be slowly. Later, Atticus explains that normally rational men are completely changed by their overwhelming racial hatred ✓ for the black community: 'Those are twelve reasonable men in everyday life, Tom's jury, but you saw something come between them and reason.' ✓

The situation is exacerbated by Tom admitting that he felt sorry for Mayella Ewell and that this is why he helped her with her chores. ✓ This is a huge mistake as it further alienates the white community, who reel in horror at the notion that a black man would have the audacity to pity a white woman. Tom realises his error, but it is too late. ✓ It is unlikely that he would have been acquitted anyway, but this reinforces to the white community that their views of 'niggers' are justified. ✓ Not even an impassioned plea from Atticus in his closing speech can save Tom.

Tom Robinson's fate was sealed the moment that Mayella Ewell accused him of rape because even though her family are looked down on as 'white trash' and generally despised, she is still white and he black. ✓ The degree of racial prejudice in Maycomb is highlighted by Atticus when he says, 'In out courts, when it's a white man's word against a black man's, the white man always wins. They're ugly, but those are the facts of life.' ✓

The people of Maycomb County have very strict ideas about what is appropriate and what is not within their society. Mr Dolphus Raymond is shunned because he has mixed-race children and Boo Radley is seen as a monster because he does not conform to the society's expectations. ✓ In such a prejudiced and judgmental society Tom stood no chance. Perhaps the one glimmer of hope is that it took the jury a few hours to decide unanimously to convict him, rather than the usual few minutes. ✓ This suggests some hope of change in the future. ✓

Examiner's comments
This is a very thorough and analytical approach to the question that takes into consideration the prevailing attitudes of the time. The candidate could have expanded on reasons behind the attitudes of the white community and mentioned that less judgmental people, such as Miss Maudie, as a woman, would not have been allowed to serve on a jury. They could also have highlighted the fact that it was a Cunningham who was at one point the only person in favour of acquitting Tom. This shows a change in attitude from the earlier incident with a Cunningham in the lynch mob.

QUICK QUIZ 1

UNCOVER THE PLOT

Jean-Louise (Scout) and her brother Jem live with their father, Atticus, and their cook, Calpurnia, in Maycomb County, Alabama. It is the 1930s, and prejudice, both racial and class-conscious, rages strongly. While Atticus practises criminal law the children spend their time at school and at play with their friend Dill. Their favourite game involves acting out the life of Arthur (Boo) Radley, a neighbour who has been shut away for so long that superstition surrounds him. As the game progresses (with Atticus's disapproval) it becomes apparent that it is not going unnoticed by someone on the Radley estate. During a night visit to the house, Jem loses his trousers: when he collects them they have been folded and inexpertly darned. Small gifts are left in the knot-hole of a Radley oak, until Boo's brother – claiming that the tree is dying – fills the hole with cement.

WHO? WHAT? WHY? WHEN? WHERE? HOW?

1 The hanging of Atticus's first two clients. Had they agreed to plead Guilty to second-degree murder he could have saved them, but they refused (1)

2 Meridian, Mississippi. His aunt, Miss Rachel Haverford, lives in Maycomb (1)

3 They kept themselves to themselves; they did not go to church (1)

4 As a disgrace. Mr Radley 'bought' his son's release with a promise to keep him out of trouble: Arthur was not seen again for 15 years (1)

5 Read and write. She cannot remember learning to read (it came to her as naturally as 'breathing'); Calpurnia taught her to write (2)

6 The Ewells. None of them worked; they lived like animals; none of the children had an education; their father was an alcoholic (8)

7 As a child who always spoke nicely to her (5)

8 'A Negro' (but really at Jem, Scout and Dill) (6)

9 When Jem decides to go back to get his trousers. Scout does not understand that Jem is less frightened by the shotgun than by the thought of Atticus's disappointment in him (6)

10 Jem understands that it was Boo who left the gifts, and that his brother knew this and disapproved. He is angry at the lie, and at the frustration of their pleasurable discoveries. Perhaps he has started to feel sorry for Boo. (7)

QUICK QUIZ 2

UNCOVER THE PLOT

For the first time since 1885 it snows in Maycomb County. During the night, Miss Maudie's house catches fire; for safety, Atticus sends Jem and Scout to stand in front of the Radley house and, while they watch the fire,

Boo Radley slips a blanket round Scout's shoulders. The children learn that their father is defending a Negro in a **difficult** case and suffer taunts from their fellows. At Christmas they go to Finch's Landing to visit their Aunt Alexandra, and Scout **fights** her cousin Francis for calling Atticus a nigger-lover. As the situation deteriorates, Jem and Scout are reminded of their father's qualities when he saves **the neighbourhood** from a mad dog by shooting it expertly and humanely – they were unaware of his shooting skills. They are tormented by Mrs Dubose, a sick neighbour, and **Jem** loses his head and ruins her camellias. As a result he is forced to read to her until shortly before her death, learning afterwards that with great courage she had fought and beaten her addiction to **morphine**.

WHO? WHAT? WHY WHEN? WHERE? HOW?

1 Jem has constructed a snowman from hardly any snow, in a very good likeness of Mr Avery (8)

2 Miss Maudie's heavy oak rocking-chair – the thing she values most (8)

3 If he didn't, he could no longer respect himself (9)

4 His parents left him with his grandparents so they could 'pursue their own pleasures' (9)

5 Uncle Jack; he didn't listen to Scout's point of view before

beating her (8)

6 The judge pointed at Atticus and said, 'You're It' (9)

7 Mockingbirds do no harm to anyone; they sing for people's pleasure (10)

8 He realised his skill gave him an unfair advantage over living things (10)

9 When Mrs Dubose says that Atticus 'laws for niggers' (11)

10 A person's conscience (11)

QUICK QUIZ 3
UNCOVER THE PLOT
Jem and Scout go to **chur**ch with Calpurnia. A collection is taken up for **Helen**, Tom Robinson's wife, because she can no longer find work. On their return they find out that Aunt Alexandra has come to live with them: her presence in the house, and Jem's new-found **maturity**, make life **uncomfortable** for Scout. Dill runs away from **home**. Tom Robinson is moved to the Maycomb jail: a group of men, led by **Walter Cunningham**, tries to 'get at' him but the tense situation is resolved when **Scout** innocently intervenes. The trial begins and Jem, Scout and Dill watch from the Negroes' **balcony**. Mayella Ewell and her father accuse Tom of having beaten Mayella and then raped her, hurting her badly on the **right side** of her face: Atticus makes it plain that the Negro, crippled in his **left** arm, could not have inflicted the injuries, and suggests that her father beat her.

Tom, Atticus's only witness, claims that Mayella attempted to seduce him. Calpurnia fetches the children home, but they return for the verdict: guilty. As Atticus leaves the courtroom, all the Negroes stand as a gesture of respect.

WHO? WHAT? WHY? WHEN? WHERE? HOW?

1 Jem (12)

2 Because her husband Tom is charged with raping a white woman (12)

3 Like the other Negroes. It aggravates people to reveal the extent of your education. You can't change them unless they want to be changed, so you can only keep silent or 'talk their language' (12)

4 Heredity (13)

5 To sack Calpurnia. Perhaps just because she is there now, and feels Calpurnia is no longer needed… but there is a suggestion that she does not like the extent to which a Negro woman is trusted and even respected in Atticus's house (14)

6 By telling Atticus that Dill has run away (14)

7 Dill does not feel wanted or needed at home; his mother and stepfather spend no time with him. Scout has always felt needed, wanted and secure (14)

8 'Do you really think so?' It usually implies that he can show the person confronting him that they are wrong. (15)

9 Jem understands how serious the situation is, but only aggravates the men by squaring up to them. Scout's innocent friendliness completely disarms Walter Cunningham (15)

10 The 'simple hell people give other people'. His reaction is instinctive when confronted with harsh reality – injustice, hypocrisy, prejudice, cruelty (20)

QUICK QUIZ 4
UNCOVER THE PLOT
The Negroes show their appreciation of what Atticus has tried to do by sending him presents of food, but the humiliated Bob Ewell spits at him and threatens him publicly. An appeal against Tom's conviction is planned, but Atticus arrives in the middle of one of Aunt Alexandra's missionary teas with the news that Tom has been shot dead trying to escape from jail. Life in Maycomb seems to settle down, although after Bob Ewell finds and loses a job, Judge Taylor is disturbed by a nocturnal visitor and Tom's widow Helen is persecuted by the Ewell family. Returning at night from a Halloween pageant, Jem and Scout are attacked. Bob Ewell is discovered dead at the scene, and it is revealed that his killer was Boo Radley, come to defend the children. The Sheriff persuades Atticus to pretend that Ewell fell on his knife, to

save Boo from public attention.

WHO? WHAT? WHY? WHEN? WHERE? HOW?

1 His eyes fill with tears (22)

2 Jem is now 'grown up' in Miss Maudie's eyes (22)

3 He knew that Tom was innocent, and that Atticus's fairness and lack of prejudice would give Tom the best chance of acquittal (22)

4 A Cunningham; Walter Cunningham was the leader of the mob that tried to lynch Tom at the jail (23)

5 Atticus (24)

6 That his action was typical of a 'nigger': cowardly, thoughtless and unplanned (25)

7 He knows that few believed his testimony (27)

8 Bob Ewell's knife when he attacks her (28)

9 His skin has hardly ever seen the sun, because he so rarely goes out (29)

10 Atticus assumes that Jem killed Bob Ewell, and he does not want to be seen to 'cover up' his son's involvement (30)

WHO SAYS

1 Jem (23)

2 Bob Ewell (27)

3 Aunt Alexandra (28)

4 Dr Reynolds (28)

5 Scout (30)

TO KILL A MOCKINGBIRD

1 Tom Robinson, who has done no harm yet ends up being shot. His good manners are perhaps like the 'music' of the mockingbird. Perhaps also Boo Radley: capable of great affection and generosity, he has been forced into seclusion

2 The public attention would be a kind of persecution for Boo

3 That she has understood the full implications of the situation and finally understands Boo's shyness

4 Think about who has been revealed as hypocritical, prejudiced, cruel, ignorant, narrow-minded. Then decide from the text whether they have more positive traits (a sense of 'fair play', a conscience, courage, the ability to learn from mistakes, etc.) Think about Aunt Alexandra, Walter Cunningham (Senior) and Mrs Dubose. Your reactions may be complicated and even inconsistent. Most of all, bear in mind the novel's humane and generous ending: ' 'Atticus, he was real nice...'... 'Most people are, Scout, when you finally see them.'

If you got all or most of these questions right you're well on your way to developing an understanding of the novel.

Good Luck in your GCSEs and whatever you do, don't panic!

Published by Letts Educational Ltd.
An imprint of HarperCollins*Publishers*
77–85 Fulham Palace Road
London W6 8JB

Telephone: 0870 787 1610
Fax: 0870 787 1720
Email: education@harpercollins.co.uk
Website: www.lettsandlonsdale.com

ISBN 9781843153139

First published 1994

Revised edition 2004

05/150610

Text © 1994 John Mahoney and Stewart Martin
2004 edition revised by Andrea Stowe

Design and illustration © Letts Educational Ltd.

Cover and text design by Hardlines Ltd., Charlbury, Oxfordshire.

Typeset by Letterpart Ltd., Reigate, Surrey.

Graphic illustration by Beehive Illustration, Cirencester, Gloucestershire.

Commissioned by Cassandra Birmingham

Editorial project management by Jo Kemp

Printed in the UK by Martins the Printers, Berwick upon Tweed

Mixed Sources
Product group from well-managed
forests and other controlled sources
www.fsc.org   Cert no. SW-COC-001806
© 1996 Forest Stewardship Council

FSC is a non-profit international organisation established to promote the
responsible management of the world's forests. Products carrying the FSC
label are independently certified to assure consumers that they come
from forests that are managed to meet the social, economic and
ecological needs of present and future generations.

Find out more about HarperCollins and the environment at
www.harpercollins.co.uk/green